ADVANCE

*The Princess Guide*

"*The Princess Guide* has a message for every young woman: There is hope for being a princess, your standards can be set on the stars, and God has a plan for your life. Moms, grandmas, aunts, and women, you need to read this book, too, because that glass slipper isn't unattainable and the hope of a sparkly ball gown isn't impossible. Remember the hope you felt as a little girl? It's revived in the pages of *The Princess Guide* in a wonderful way."

—Sarah Reinhard, author of *A Catholic Mother's
Companion to Pregnancy*

"What does it mean to be a princess? And why do countless little girls, regardless of time and culture, long to become one? In *The Princess Guide*, Jennessa Terraccino helps readers discern that being a princess is about much more than finding Prince Charming and living happily ever after. It's about becoming who we were all made to be: daughters of the King. This book connects the dots between little girls' fantasies and grown women's desires, finding kernels of truth at the heart of familiar fairy tales. For parents wondering what to make of their daughter's princess obsession and for young women wondering when their prince will come, *The Princess Guide* weaves timely insights into timeless tales about the feminine vocation and the search for true love."

—Emily Stimpson, author of *These Beautiful Bones:
An Everyday Theology of the Body*

"Young women are thrust into a culture today that's eager to push the boundaries of previous generations. With progress has come great license: the guardrails have come off, and girls have little to help them navigate the turbulent waters of adolescence and early adulthood. *The Princess Guide* serves as a manual for young women longing to find relationships that last, where they are honored and cherished without having to compromise their dignity and inner beauty along the way. Used as a reference or read straight through, the author propels the reader with the fuel of her 'theology of fairy tales' to embrace her unmistakable role as the princess of her own unfolding tale."

—Elsa Rose Hoffmann, executive director of
Pure Fashion, Washington, DC

THE PRINCESS GUIDE

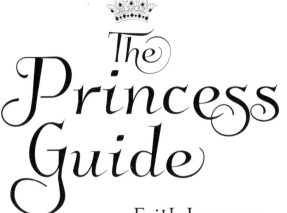

# The Princess Guide

Faith Lessons
*from*
Snow White,
Cinderella &
Sleeping Beauty

JENNESSA
TERRACCINO

servant
AN IMPRINT OF
FRANCISCAN MEDIA
Cincinnati, Ohio

Scripture quotations are from *The Revised Standard Version of the Bible: Catholic Edition*, copyright © 1965, 1966 the Division of Christian Education of the National Council of the Churches of Christ in the United States of America. Used by permission. All rights reserved. Scripture texts marked NAB in this work are taken from the *New American Bible*, revised edition © 2010, 1991, 1986, 1970 Confraternity of Christian Doctrine, Washington, D.C., and are used by permission of the copyright owner. All rights reserved.

LIBRARY OF CONGRESS CATALOGING-IN-PUBLICATION DATA
Terraccino, Jennessa.
The princess guide : faith lessons from Snow White, Cinderella, and Sleeping Beauty / Jennessa Terraccino ; foreword by Teresa Tomeo.
pages cm
Summary: "The Princess Guide uses fairy tales—specifically the stories of three princesses (Snow White, Cinderella, and Sleeping Beauty)—to inspire young women to dignity, femininity, and fervent faith. With a timeless yet relevant voice, it explores issues important to women today. Scenes from the fairy tales are the backdrop for a new way to look at beauty, vocation, sexuality and chastity, modesty in fashion, and friendship. Personal stories and passages from Scripture, the wisdom of the saints, and the Catechism of the Catholic Church help you discover the princess within»— Provided by publisher.
Includes bibliographical references and index.
ISBN 978-1-61636-851-7 (paperback : acid-free paper)
1. Fairy tales—History and criticism. 2. Christianity in literature. 3. Young women in literature. 4. Femininity in literature. 5. Princesses in literature. 6. Women—Folklore. I. Title.
PN3437.T45 2015
398.2—dc23
2014037892

ISBN 978-1-61636-851-7

Published by Servant Books, an imprint of
Franciscan Media.
28 W. Liberty St.
Cincinnati, OH 45202
www.FranciscanMedia.org

Printed in the United States of America.
Printed on acid-free paper.
15 16 17 18 19  5 4 3 2 1

# Contents

*To*

MARY, MOST HOLY QUEEN

*and*

THE OUR LADY OF HOPE

YOUTH GROUP LADIES

# Foreword

As women we can tell ourselves all we want that princess fairy tales—whether they involve Cinderella, Snow White, Sleeping Beauty, or all of the above—are just that: fairy tales. But deep down we still want the fairy-tale ending. We might not expect the castle or the glass slippers, but we certainly want the handsome prince.

This was very evident to me when I took my great-niece to a Disney on Ice show. This particular event featured the main characters of many of the Disney movies, several based on those timeless fairy tales we know and love. As we entered the arena to take our seats, I noticed that most of the young girls in the audience were dressed in their favorite Disney princess getups. And even though plenty of male heroes would also be taking to the ice that evening, it was mostly the little girls who were all decked out in princess attire. Some of the little boys wielded a fake sword here or plastic shield there, but the boys weren't nearly as committed to playing the part as the girls. The little girls were dressed like princesses from head to toe including the crowns, the gowns, and any other items that would add more glitz and glamour to their princess bling.

As a media expert, I am well aware of the influence that the culture—and in particular Madison Avenue—can have on consumers, especially the youngest consumers among us. I'm not naïve enough to think that the marketing that goes along with today's most popular animated movies has little or no effect. That said, I am also a Christian who is well aware that deep down we are made for love and relationship—relationship with God and each other. We long to be loved; that desire to be adored and treated like royalty is in our DNA. Call me crazy, but I think it is that desire and not the latest TV spot or billboard that is causing little Sally or Cindy to dress up like her royal highness.

That's why I believe *The Princess Guide* will resonate with today's woman no matter her state in life. First of all, this book will take us back to simpler times when we were children—when there was little more to worry about than what bedtime story Mom or Dad was going to read to us that night or what we were going to wear to school the next day. Given the frantic, even frenetic, lifestyles we lead, how comforting is it to remember what it was like to actually have time to play, read, and visit imaginary lands where everyone lives happily ever after?

Second, this princess guide shows us how art imitates life. By taking a closer look at some of the conversations of Snow White, Cinderella, and Sleeping Beauty, we can see that, although the stories and subsequent movie scripts may have been written for children, the writers no doubt knew it would touch adult hearts and minds as well. Why? Because truth is truth. Truth does not change with the times. The simple life's lessons learned by the fictional royalty can be applied to our own journey as well.

Sometimes, thanks to the baggage we carry, even though we long to be treated like princesses, we just can't see ourselves good enough to wear a crown. Despite what we may have attained in life in terms of an education, a good job, and even a family, many of us still struggle with low self-esteem. Maybe we see our past mistakes or current problems as real road blocks to our true royal heritage. Or maybe we keep comparing ourselves to other women around us and just can't convince ourselves that we are princess material.

That's one of the reasons this book is so important. Jennessa helps us see that God doesn't make junk. He makes real-life princesses. Happily ever after is the reality that a very special prince wants for all of his children, and in particular his daughters. We are all daughters of the Prince of Peace and the King of Kings. It sounds too good to be true, but God willing, when we get to heaven, we might even find a castle or two—a mansion with many rooms, to be more precise.

"In my Father's house are many rooms. If it were not so, would I have told you that I go to prepare a place for you?" (John 14:2). Mansions with lots of rooms and a feast, fit for a King and his royal subjects—you guessed it, you and me.

So brush off the tiara. Grab the beaded ball gown from the attic. Read how fairy tales do really come true. The love of God conquers all—and your chariot ride to his kingdom awaits.

—*Teresa Tomeo*

# Introduction

## ONCE UPON A TIME...

O nce I had the joy of catching a glimpse of a petite princess. Weaving through the aisles of the grocery store, I came upon a cart, and in this cart sat a little girl, all decked out in princess regalia. As she glided by, her cart served as her carriage. Her legs barely fit through the designated holes due to the obstruction of abundant pink tulle that blossomed forth from her shiny, rose-colored dress. While I was glued to the reality of my errand, she daydreamed from her metal-wire throne. Surely, the thoughts that filled her mind were as sparkly as her silver, sequined crown.

Seeing this little girl all dressed up tickled me pink, not just because she was wearing a lot of pink, but because this little girl knew herself to be a princess—something many young women, who were once girls, have forgotten all about. Most ladies choose not to display their princess hearts so publicly, but cannot deny that they remain royalty deep down. While the world today encourages women to forget these soulful desires, the enchantment, nevertheless, continues (even if it is secret). To be a princess is not a phase or a fashion; instead, it is something stamped upon every woman's soul.

What girl from a very young age hasn't had an attraction to fairy tales involving princesses? Just the other day, I found myself in a bookstore in the children's literature corner. One precious girl, who was four years old or so, was reading (or simply reciting from memory) a princess tale aloud in a whispery way. She then asked her mom if she could have the book. Her mom responded, "I think we have enough princess books. How about something different?" You see, even in this modern world, little ladies have an attraction to princesses, a yearning to be a daughter-turned-damsel. Yet sometimes we grown-up ladies have allowed our desire for a royal title to fade away.

I have always loved princess stories. I began to be enamored with "Once upon a times" when I fell asleep reading my first copy of *Sleeping Beauty*, whimsically becoming Sleeping Beauty myself in my dreams. From then on, I yearned to be known as a princess—and in time realized I actually *was* one! Is that so crazy to believe? No, I wasn't born noble, but I was adopted into royalty through baptism. All Christians are: "For in Christ Jesus you are all sons (and daughters) of God, through faith" (Galatians 3:26). God is known as a king (Psalm 145), so if we are his daughters, that would make us...yup, royal heirs! "We are children of God, and if children then heirs, heirs of God and fellow heirs with Christ" (Romans 8:16–17).

Also, the Blessed Mother is known as a queen: "And a great portent appeared in heaven, a woman clothed with the sun, with the moon under her feet, and on her head a *crown* of twelve stars" (Revelation 12:1, emphasis added). If Mary, the Mother of God, is a queen, and we also invoke her as our mother, we, as daughters, can certainly own the princess title.

If we do this, however, it means owning up to all that a princess represents. Such expectations of behavior will be revealed throughout the chapters of this book. One little friend of mine, just two and a half years old, has already discovered her calling, which is the calling of every woman. She summarized it shortly and sweetly when she said to me, "I am a princess, a queen, and a girl." She gets it, but do we? Maybe it's time to illuminate how to live out what is already written on our hearts.

As I recognized this royal reality for myself, my vision began to be shaped, and I embraced what I like to call a "theology of fairy tales." These timeless stories hold great symbolism. Our heavenly Father's fingerprints are everywhere, and this world is an arrow that points to him. In reviewing my favorite princess stories, I began to see a greater meaning present. For these chronicles hold a deeper reality in light of Christ. From the beginning of time, humans were was created in the image and likeness of God (Genesis 1:27); therefore, not only does man reflect God in himself, but all that man does and designs has the potential to reflect God, as well—even fairy stories.

Fairy tales "contain many things besides elves and fays, and besides dwarfs, witches, trolls, giants, or dragons: [they hold] the seas, the sun, the moon, the sky; and the earth, and all that are in it: tree and bird, water and stone, wine and bread, and ourselves, mortal men, when we are enchanted."[1] So let us dive deeply into such chronicles. May we be enthralled with the path of princesses, so that we too may be contained in the story that is already on our hearts. It is time to make the road our own—and see what we find along the journey.

In reality, in God's embrace is where a woman's hearts belongs. In Christ, a woman is home. He is royalty, and we are coheirs: princesses, queens, and girls. It is in understanding divine revelation that a woman begins to make sense of herself, the world around her, and even fairy tales. Just as Sleeping Beauty awakes from a slumber, when a young woman begins to embrace Christ, she awakens from her dormancy. The world is new to her because she sees it differently. She becomes a bride of Christ, and the veil from her is lifted.

Just the other day, I bought a new pair of sunglasses. Of course they had rhinestone clusters on the side. Before now, I had never really worn sunglasses, but figured it was better to protect my eyes. One thing I have noticed when wearing sunglasses is that you can often see the sky's amazing designs better. Picture those mornings when rays of light reach out through the clouds, stretching to earth. The majestic glowing beams, in their greatness, remind me of God's fingers. Without my eye apparel, these columns of light were dull, blending into the sky. But with the sunglasses on, I could see the contrast so clearly, and it brought me to a moment where I contemplated God: his might and his love. It was like wearing Christ-colored glasses. When you live a life in Christ, you see his fingerprints more clearly, not just in the sky but in every aspect of life.

Fairy tales can be like those sunglasses, allowing us to see God with new vision and insight. Overall, "the value of myth is that it takes all the things you know and restores to them the rich significance which has been hidden by the veil of familiarity."[2] The mysteries of such tales can bring us to a greater understanding of our faith—and our femininity, as it was designed by our Creator. We are no different from Snow White, Cinderella, or Sleeping Beauty, who at first did not know they were princesses. Through a journey, each was awakened, and then knew who they truly were. Come awake, dear sister, come alive! Open your eyes. The regal is real, and you wear the crown.

Wait...did you hear that? In the distance now I hear the faint sound of a trumpet blast. The invitations are being carried to each fair maiden in the kingdom. When the knock on your door comes, the carrier will hand you a scroll, and the thick paper will read:

*Dear Princess,*

*At this very moment in time, you, my beauty, are now invited to put on your Christ-colored lenses and your glass slippers for the journey ahead. I pray you will join me by allowing me to rescue you. May my love and vision for your life truly envelop you—and help you to see yourself as the exquisite princess you were always created to be.*

*Love,*

*Your Prince,*

*Jesus*

Are you ready?

# Part One

• ~ • ~ •

## SNOW WHITE

"She was as white as snow, with lips as red as blood,
and her hair was black as ebony."[1]
—*The Brothers Grimm*

• ~ • ~ •

# Chapter One

## MIRROR, MIRROR ON THE WALL
### ~ Beauty ~

E very young woman, if she is honest with herself, will admit that the word "beautiful" is often on her mind. Continually, she finds herself tossing about the question, "Am I beautiful?"—a question that motivates her actions, launching a routine of reflective glances. Whether at home, in the car, or in a passing shop window, she finds herself staring back in a glassy gaze as she internally questions, "Mirror, mirror on the wall, who's the fairest of them all?"

You may recall the opening of *Snow White*. One of the first characters we meet is the crowned Queen. She is fierce, and, yes, she appears beautiful. Her obsession with beauty is deep, though her actual beauty is not. Her heart is afflicted with a diseased question. She, who models woman's insecurity, interrogates the fire-filled mirror and asks, "Mirror, Mirror, on the wall, who in this land is the fairest of them all?"[1] Certainly, this is a question that has entered our own thoughts, but from where does this unsettling query arise?

Well, it began with one woman. Her name? Eve. Just as the Queen speaks with something known as her slave, Eve spoke with a serpent that tried to enslave. And every woman since then has done so. Eve must have been stunningly beautiful. After all, she, like all of us, was made in the image and likeness of God (see Genesis 1:26). Without a doubt, beauty is one of God's many attributes, and I am sure Eve reflected it through a pure, untouched exquisiteness. Yet, she ached to obtain something more, and, with some light convincing, she became sure that God was holding out on her.

Once she eats, and defies the heavenly King, the battle between good and evil is set in motion. Eve's vision is forever tainted, and a fatal fountain of curses springs forth. Instantly, she is ashamed of herself, and questions, "Am I beautiful?" Doubting, she hides her naked self. God finds her still, and when he does, he has a lot to say. In the midst of a list of repercussions, God says to the Serpent, "I will put enmity between you and the woman" (Genesis 3:15). What does that mean for Eve and any young woman? Satan is forever her antagonist. He hates her, and he rivals God for her heart. He whispers words of doubt and temptations to the soul, and he seeks to make her ill-willed toward God and others. And the worst part is that he's not so obvious about his actions. He's a trickster. Subtle, polluted thoughts and ideas are always in the mind, sprouting forth from the enemy's secret prompt- ings. All of this creates quite the drama, in which a woman is at war with herself and other women. How much we have bought into the lies that Satan feeds. For every woman, it is a daily struggle to identify one's own beauty—and assess how it measures up to others'.

We see this in *Snow White*. The mirror does not affirm the Queen in her unspoken desire to be "most beautiful." Instead, to the Queen's query, the mirror says: "Young Snow White...she is most fair. For none with her beauty will ever compare."[2] She "who was as white as snow, with lips as red as blood, and whose hair was as black as ebony."[3]

What a scene! Can you feel the intense passion building in her heart?

Once the Queen feels that her beauty is under attack, she seeks to exterminate the threat. What does she ask, but for the assigned assassin to bring back Snow White's heart? Just like the enemy, Satan, she is after the heart.

Is it like this in your community? Unlike guys, ladies are not as prone to break out in a fistfight, but they have been known to demoralize the heart of their projected rival. First, there are the silent glances filled with judgment: "I'll glance at her earrings and recognize that they are cute, but not affirm her." You know the destructive mind games that you play over a girl who makes you question your own beauty. Soon, soundless snobbery results in a vindictive verbal exchange filled with jealous talk designed to demoralize. By deflating someone else, we hope to inflate ourselves, especially at times when we feel threatened by another woman's skills, status, stuff, or splendor. However, it is wise to embrace the words of St. Jerome, who said, "The face is the mirror of the mind, and a woman's eyes without a word betray the secrets of her heart."[4] If your mind isn't producing a good reflection, it is time to purify it.

Thus, we cannot continue in harshness, whether in thought, facial expression, or deed. Nor can we continue in vain self-focus. It's time to break the curse. Time to stop picking rotten fruit from the wrong tree and start picking life-giving fruit from the tree of life. You haven't forgotten about that tree, have you? Along with the tree of knowledge of good and evil, a second tree was also there in the garden. "And out of the ground the Lord God made to grow every tree that is pleasant to the sight and good for food, the tree of life also in the midst of the garden" (Genesis 2:9). That tree still remains; it is Christ upon the cross, with his arms outstretched to you, ready to embrace you, ready to forgive you, ready to redeem you, ready to love you. Christ is food for your soul.

Conversion from the curse of sin is imperative. We cannot live in our old ways and expect to be made new in Christ. A good conversion story is that of killer of Christians Saul-turned-to-Paul on the road to Damascus. It was there that Christ began to do his work in him (Acts 9:1–31), when he was given new vision. The worldly veil was lifted—he did not just wear Christ-colored lenses, he had corrective Christ-colored laser eye surgery. In Scripture we read, "And immediately something like scales fell from his eyes and he regained his sight. Then he rose and was baptized" (Acts 9:18). When St. Paul was changed, his conversion prompted action: He was immediately baptized. If we accept Christ into our hearts, then we too need to be motivated to act, to grow, to change.

Though St. Paul was not a woman, he definitely has a lot of wisdom to share with the ladies. For instance, he speaks about what women should focus on: "Women should adorn themselves…not with braided hair or gold or pearls or costly attire but by good deeds" (1 Timothy 2:9–10). I assure you he isn't saying you should wear a potato sack jumper and stop plucking your eyebrows. It is not bad to dress in a stylish way, but it is truly in vain if all of a lady's energy is spent beautifying the exterior while neglecting her soul. Thus, he is encouraging each young woman to gaze more upon Christ and less on herself. Don't throw out your mirror, but make sure you aren't lingering in its shallowness. As Fulton Sheen said, "The more the soul is clothed with virtue, the less is the need for outer compensation."[5] Seek a true and deeper reflection, the one where you reflect Christ in all that you are and all that you do. Stop asking the question, "Am I beautiful?" and become truly beautiful in Christ. Don't hide like Eve in doubt and darkness. Halt the hunt for a superficial beauty that will fade, and instead stand before Christ and let Jesus affirm you in your beauty.

We all have imperfections turned to insecurities that plague us, leading us to doubt our beauty, and so we often seek an *unattainable* physical perfection. In reality, our imperfection should lead us to what is perfect, but this perfection is found outside of ourselves. This perfection is Christ himself. In him, even our bodies will be transformed. "Just as we have borne the image of the man of dust, we shall also bear the image of the man of heaven" (1 Corinthians 15:49). Our resurrected body will be incorruptible and glorious (1 Corinthians 15:42–43). In fact, on earth we have a foreshadowing of this in the saints known as the "incorruptibles," saints whose bodies did not know the normal decay of death even after burial.

One of these saints is St. Bernadette, who had visions of the Blessed Mother under the title of the "Immaculate Conception" in Lourdes, France. St. Bernadette became a religious sister at a young age, and soon after passed away at the age of twenty-three from a terrible illness. Thirty years after her burial, her body was exhumed by the Church to find her exactly as she was on the day of her death. Her body now rests in the Convent of Saint-Gildard at Nevers, which is open to the public. Much like Snow White, St. Bernadette remains in a crystal and gold-clad coffin. Call her a sleeping saint who awaits her true prince, Jesus. It is as if her resting body is sharing this verse with all of us, "My flesh will dwell in hope…for thou wilt not abandon my soul to Hades nor let the Holy one see corruption" (Acts 2:26–27). Who needs anti-aging cream when you have Jesus? Our hope and beauty are in the resurrected Christ! Jesus will "change our lowly body to be like his glorious body, by the power which enables him even to subject all things to himself" (Philippians 3:21).

If you only really need one mirror, Jesus Christ, isn't it time to get rid of the others? What else serves as your "mirror on the wall"? Who and what do you seek in order to be affirmed in your beauty? Is it the oh-so-popular girls? A herd of guys at your school? A particular crush? Fashion magazines? The celebrity cult of music artists, actresses, and models? Past memories of the times you were mocked? Do you look to society to tell you what is, who is, and if you are beautiful? Like any mirror, these reflectors of society will draw our attention, but please know they will lie to you. These mirrors open a portal of comparison, which will only make you lust for beauty more, leaving you insecure in your own skin.

So, are you after the standards of society or the standards of saints? Society's focus is on the outward appearance, offering you an endless array of products that all come with promises. It tells you what to wear and what to show. It tells you what shape to be and which shade to color your hair. Society offers a restless chase for beauty because it constantly whispers, "What you are is never good enough." There is always another product to have, another pound to lose, and a new style to possess. *Stop!* That's not how Jesus sees things at all. "For the Lord sees not as man sees; man looks on the outward appearance, but the Lord looks on the heart" (1 Samuel 16:7). And in Song of Solomon he sings to you, saying, "Behold, you are beautiful, my love, / behold, you are beautiful" (4:1). Soak it in!

After all, what makes Snow White beautiful? Yes, she has been blessed with an exterior beauty, but there is something more profound to her loveliness, which dwells in her heart. No matter how Snow White was dressed, rags and all, she was striking. What is her beauty secret? It is grace! It was not the exterior but truly the interior that allowed her to outshine the Queen in splendor. "The less beauty the soul has, the more it needs to decorate the body."[6] Besides Snow White, there is another woman to look to for authentic beauty tips: Mary, who is "full of grace"

(Luke 1:28). Certainly, the Blessed Mother is a womanly example for all of us to follow. "She is what every woman wants to be when she looks at herself.... She is the way every woman wants to command respect and love because the beauty of her goodness of body and soul."[7] Our Lady "found favor with God" (Luke 1:30), and we should seek to do the same by living a life in Christ, one of virtue and of grace. "We often forget that Mary was human like us. She understands our struggles, fears, and pains. She experienced the same things—but she always remained open to the love and grace of God and she always said yes to him."[7] Like Eve, the Queen lusts for beauty. Like Mary, Snow White possesses innate beauty. What example will you follow: the path Eve walked to death or the way of life Mary found when she welcomed Christ to make a home in her (see *CCC* 494)? Eve turned away from God, while Mary turned toward God. Eve consumed bad fruit, while Mary bore blessed fruit. "Blessed are you among women, and blessed is the fruit of your womb" (Luke 1:42). Virtue is a step toward cultivating authentic beauty, for the love and grace that is within a woman is what truly shines through to make her radiant. Grace illuminates the exterior. To gain this grace, Mary is your guide; pray the Hail Mary. For a meditation on true beauty, recite it devoutly with emphasis on the words "full of grace" and with the intention of integrating such grace into your life because it dwells deeply in your soul.

A friend of mine once shared with me a fitting analogy about stained glass windows. Such windows are beautiful, but this beauty is dull without light beams bursting through them to make them brilliant. He said, "We are the glass. Christ is the light." Jesus shines through us and heightens our beauty. This is how Snow White and Our Lady possess beauty. Without Christ, darkness dulls and defeats, leaving us lackluster—stained glass without a light source. Vice and lust for beauty ultimately lead to ugliness. In the end, the Queen's wrinkled and aged appearance accurately mirrors her ugliness within; her interior became her exterior. "The wickedness of a wife changes her appearance, / and darkens her face like that of a bear" (Sirach 25:17).

Therefore, "let not yours be the outward adorning...but let it be the hidden person of the heart with the imperishable jewel of a gentle and quiet spirit, which in God's sight is very precious" (1 Peter 3:3–4). Look to heaven to be affirmed in your beauty. God's standards for you are worth pursuing. Replace your old mirrors with Christ, Scripture's words, and women of virtue, including the Queen of Heaven and God-fearing friends who will support you in your endeavor to reflect true beauty.

Last, realize that there is not a "fairest of them all." I remember the first time that hit me. I was in seventh grade, and it was the opening night of the school play, *Knights of the Rad Table*, and I stood in the greenroom, where all the actors and actresses dress the part of their character before going on stage. A large mirror lined one of the walls, and I studied the faces that stood in it. Makeup was being applied to their features. In particular, the faces of two girls struck me, for I noticed that both were truly beautiful, but so very different from each other. That night, my vision of beauty expanded by realizing in that moment that there was not one "beautiful."

I did not have to covet their beauty, resent them, or try to verbally lessen them. They were beautiful, and so was I, and so are all women. There is no need to mirror someone else. In that moment backstage, peace filled my heart. Now whenever I feel envy sprouting, I defuse it by offering true affirmation to the one by whom I feel freshly challenged. We all need to band together to affirm each other, recognizing that we are all beautiful. And we need to aid each other in cultivating authentic beauty in a culture that only has counterfeits to offer. Instead of getting caught up in tearing other ladies down in thought or deed, sprinkle affirmation on others throughout your day, and everyone will feel more beautiful. Hey, who doesn't like sprinkles?

# Chapter Two

## I LOVE YOU MORE THAN ANYTHING
### ~ *Soul Mates* ~

Apparently, a lot of romances begin in gardens. This has not been the case for me personally. In fact, I am more of a garden avoider—with good reason.

Maybe it is because I once had to garden in high heels; those shoes were never the same after that. My job title was "administrative assistant," which I found out on the first day was just a fancy name for a "miscellaneous helper." Apparently, part of what I was administering was the courtyard garden.

My next garden affair was self-motivated, as one spring I decided it was time to break out the rake and do some garden cleanup in our petite suburban yard. I managed to fill a huge trash bin with crusty leaves, but then things got a little too exciting—I swept the rake over the last area, a snake shot out at me. Alarmed, I dropped the rake and ran up the sidewalk, making an impractical promise to never garden again. A few months later, I tried to rectify my prior garden engagements by planting flowers. This time I had a few worm encounters, but I would have preferred to have a *warm* encounter, which gets us back to those garden romances.

The very first romance to take place in a garden was the world's very first romance—between Adam and Eve. As you know, God first made

Adam, but soon realized that "it is not good that the man should be alone" (Genesis 2:18). God had made many amazing creatures, but not one struck Adam at the heart because none were like him. You know the rest of the scene: Adam falls asleep, and Eve is created using one of his ribs.

But that's not the part on which I want to focus. Instead, let's back up for a moment. Right after God said "It is not good that the man should be alone," another important and beautiful line follows: "I will make him a helper fit for him" (Genesis 2:18). God, who just created the world out of nothing, who obviously has the power to do anything, doesn't create several women. Instead, he makes one, *just* one—the perfect fit. God knows his son Adam so intimately that he already knows who his soul mate should be. And if God is capable of making a perfect fit for Adam, that would lead one to believe he is capable of the same for all of his sons and daughters.

In the book of Tobit, we read another example of God's generosity in directing man and woman together. Tobias comes to understand that he is called to marry a lovely young lady named Sarah. However, it is known that previous suitors have not been successful at taking her as a bride. In fact, things went so badly that they, well, died (check out chapters 6—8 for the details). You can imagine Tobias is not buying into this as a match, but the archangel Raphael comes to him and says, "Do not be afraid, for she was destined for you from eternity" (Tobit 6:18). Through a noble pursuit, Sarah becomes Tobias's helper. How beautiful to think God the Father had a specific person in mind for both Tobias and Sarah, and in his proper time, against all odds, he brought them together in union. Thus, why not believe that God has someone very specific in mind for you?

Indeed, part of the drama of life is the yearning that we all feel for a soul mate. Guys tend to be on girls' minds a lot: Ladies talk about the guys they know and the kind of guy they'd like to end up with someday. Hidden away in the pages of a girl's diary is most likely a list. What's on this list? A collection of thoughts on the virtues, skills, personality, and appearance that she hopes a spouse will possess. It is important to prayerfully record the desires of the heart, always remembering that you are destined for union with someone very special, your perfect fit, and you have no need to settle. But, it is also good not to be obsessive or superstitious about the list. As you mature and grow, you should reevaluate the list that you've made, while questioning who is at work—you or God? In doing this, your pondering of these desires will be rooted in holiness.

I cannot tell you how many times I thought I had found the one. This is often the case in the sweep of infatuation that fills us when we just meet someone new. Almost instantly, we are convinced that our soul mate has been found. Our list can help guide us to be true to the desires that rest on our hearts, but make sure the list doesn't turn into a paper snowman. Unlike the traditional snowman, it is not made with snow; rather, with yellow sticky notes. On each note is a characteristic, and when this snowman faces the wind, all the paper blows away and is scattered. Such a man is a mere invention of the mind, and sets us up for disappointment. We cannot *make* a man out of characteristics, but we can find a man who *possesses* many of the qualities for which we long. Moreover, we need to realize that the things on our list are not everything. So don't get rid of the list, but put it in God's hands and be open to his possibility for you. His vision and understanding of the love he desires for you will amaze you. Will you allow him to show you?

Snow White may not have been one to keep lists in journals, but she did express herself and her heart's secrets by singing. Where do we first find Snow White singing her heart out? In a *garden*, while she hovers over a well and doves join her. Her lyrical lines about meeting her prince suggest that she too has one love embossed upon her heart. Coincidently, her audience shares the same belief, as turtledoves are known for taking only one partner and are faithful to that mate for a lifetime.[1]

While working in the garden, Snow White expresses her hope that he will find her. She may be preparing herself for him, but she is going about her duties while being available. There is a desire for union, but she does not lust for it. The trend to *true* love, as we'll continue to see, is that of princely pursuit—and find her he does. Prince Ferdinand hurdles over the garden wall and sings some notes of his own, with words telling us he has been searching for his helpmate, and that his everlasting love is meant only for Snow White.[2] Again, this theme of one continues—another soul mate found in a garden. Just as Adam recognized Eve, saying, "This at last is bone of my bones / and flesh of my flesh" (Genesis 2:23), so Prince Ferdinand recognizes his bride-to-be. He declares, "I love you more than everything in the world; come with me to my father's palace. You shall be my wife."[3] So, too, can we hope to distinguish our one true love. Believe in God's faithfulness and plans for you. "The heart has its own secret melody, and one day when the score is played the heart answers, 'This is it.'"[4] Throughout your life, you will meet a lot of people. Many will be attractive to you or find you attractive. You may go through a cycle of crushes, but in the end, seek to recognize *God's* choice for you. Sometimes we decide on the guy for us, but in reality we need to be open to God's plan and trust that he knows who will best suit us. After all, God is the Father of all, and he intimately knows all of his children, making him the perfect matchmaker. Most definitely, he has someone in mind for you, and if you ask, he will help you determine just who that is. Be prayerful, and surrender your spouse selection to Jesus. This takes time and patience, and it might mean you have more dates with your girlfriends.

If we were made for one, why do we get mixed up with so many? One reason is that we are impatient. We don't feel like waiting on the Lord, so we climb down from the tower and pursue. Perhaps we are simply excited about dating, so we date the cute crush that is before us for fun. Dating becomes a hobby of collecting has-beens instead of truly searching for a husband.

Another possible reason is that we feel bad saying no, so we settle. Or maybe we want someone to recognize our beauty, and we think we will gain this affirmation through dating. Along the way, we might have figured out that the guy we are with is not the one, but our hearts are invested, and that makes it tough to walk away. We get emotionally attached. Despite the emotions that push and pull at our hearts, it is worth waiting on the Lord's ideal in order to keep our hearts unscathed. Until then, be a garden locked (see Song of Solomon 4:12–16).

Just like Adam and Eve, Snow White and the prince are not exactly alone in the garden. There is a unique object at the center of the garden: a well.[5] Now, I am not superstitious, and I don't believe in wishing wells, but I do think that this well can extend our thoughts to the important topic of love. You may be asking what a well has to do with love. Well, a lot. You see, the love between two people is incomplete. In actuality, it takes "three to make love."[6] Love must look outside itself; it must look to God. After all, "God is love" (1 John 4:8), and he must be the source of their love. "Two glasses that are empty cannot fill up one another. There must be a fountain of water outside the glasses, in order that they may have communion with one another."⁷ So, let us look at this well as a symbol of Christ. Christ must always be in our garden. We must draw upon him in order to truly love. When God is taken out of the equation, we are depriving ourselves of a deep richness and are setting our relationship up for failure. Without a well, our relationships will soon go dry.

So, a symbol of Christ is present in the scene, but someone else is there, too. You see, I am not the only one who finds snakes in gardens. Adam and Eve's love was torn apart by the snake known as Satan. He was ever waiting to destroy what God had built between two souls. The enemy is present in Snow White's garden, too. This time he takes the form of a wicked Queen glaring down at the two from a balcony window. She is seeking to come between Snow White and Prince Ferdinand—and to ultimately destroy their love.

As you explore your own relationships, be sure to keep your eyes open to what is in your garden, to discern who and what is in your midst. Welcome Christ into your relationships, and draw upon him. Ask him to prepare you for, guide you to, and help you recognize your soul mate. Trust in his timing and his delivery. You just never know when that prince might hurtle over a wall. Waiting takes patience, but you won't regret waiting for the right one.

If you are dating someone now, don't be too quick to peg him as the one. If you have heavy doubts, avoid trying to convince yourself that the man you are dating is your soul mate if he is not. The longer you hold on to him, the longer you are keeping each other from your true soul mates. Ask Jesus to protect you from wrong decisions and the wicked one, and make sure you are looking at reality. How? First, stay on your knees in prayer. Is peace present in your heart? Do you feel like you are settling? What do your parents and friends say? If they see something you don't, it is possible you to need to look at your relationship with greater discernment. The enemy might not be so obviously known to you, but that does not mean he is not tampering. Don't be afraid to do some weeding to remove any unwelcome guests. In the meantime, as you wait, throw yourself into your mission at hand, whether it is school, work, or something else entirely. And never give up trusting and lifting your desires to your heavenly King.

# Chapter Three

## SHE WAS SO TERRIFIED
### ~ *Fear* ~

F ew things wake me up in the middle of the night. However, there are those summer nights when the strong rhythm of thunder can startle anyone out of slumber. You may be nestled under the covers, but when the crack from the heavens above is heard in surround sound, you do not feel so safe. For a moment, you may even forget where you are, as your mind struggles to push through the thickness of sleep into alarmed awareness. Finger-like flashes of bold light add to the unexpected anxiety, and pelting raindrops and pelting raindrops create an ominous melody . We feel quite small and out of control.

If only such storms were isolated to the weather. Instead, often our bodies rumble with the effects of storms that spread from the hub of the heart. In a moment of emotional fury, tears become a woman's words, as she seems to forget how to communicate in any other way. We have all been there. At times, our story can become a series of clouds and crosses. Storms happen: a friendship turned bitter, a bad breakup, rude or hurtful comments, a failing grade, getting cut from the team, a car accident, the death of a loved one, a poor choice, or insert the name of your current inner storm. At the core of these trials rests fear.

Even in the land of fairy tales, things did not always go perfectly. One moment Princess Snow White is picking flowers on a lovely day, most likely contemplating the handsome prince she met just the day before. Things are going well in her world. But then, suddenly suffering greets her with the sour smell of a stalker who comes her way, seeking to strike. In this scene from *Snow White* the shadowy one is after her heart with a dagger. A blade is about to wound her flesh, when Snow White receives a breath of aid. In panic-like remorse, the appointed assassin shouts at her to run away and hide.[1] Fear causes us to run.

In all my days of watching sports, I've never seen anyone sprint so fast in heels. Despite Snow White's best effort, the wilderness seems to consume her. She "was all alone in the great forest, and so terrified."[2] She leaves one storm just to face another, as her running leads her down a trail of tears and fears. She is embraced by cascading terror: a dark wooded curtain filled with glowing eyes, branches that reach to hook bodies, faces that appear in the base of bark, spider webs that lead the way to a deep pit where wood planks appear as gators.[3] Her response? Fear, not faith; exhausted, she screams and then collapses, inwardly and outwardly, and cries. I think most ladies might have the same response. Storms can be overwhelming, halting, and emotional draining.

Without a doubt, you were not the first to experience a trial. Even those closest to Jesus during his time on earth faced storms; in fact, one in particular comes to mind. After a long day of performing miracles and teaching through parables, Jesus ends up by the sea, and the disciples and Jesus depart by boat to retreat from the crowd. Jesus easily slips into sleep—and sunshine is soon swallowed by a storm. "And behold, there arose a great storm on the sea, so that the boat was being swamped by the waves" (Matthew 8:24). Under the intensity of the sea, the apostles are sure that they are sinking and convinced they will expire under the weight of waves. While Jesus is sleeping, the disciples are freaking out! With the rising water, fear also rises in the heart of each of them. Moreover, they begin to doubt that Jesus cares. They wake him and say, "Teacher, do you not care if we perish" (Mark 4:38)? At once, Jesus calms the sea, turns to the disciples, and asks, "Why are you afraid, have you no faith?" (Mark 4:40). This question is for us, too. Clearly, Jesus is in charge of all things, having the power to calm even nature's most brutal threats. The disciples are in awe.

The funny thing about their reaction is this is not the first miracle of Jesus's they have witnessed. In fact, *just that day*, Jesus had cured many from disease and illness, including Peter's mother-in-law (Matthew 8:1–17). But, in an instant, all the good Jesus has done is forgotten. Have we forgotten the good Jesus has done in our own lives? One moment, we are caught up in celebration with candles lit, and the next we are left in the dark due to a full-cheeked windy sweep across the flames. Face it: Our faith can be as fickle as a candle flame, which *we* blow out. When the darkness hits, do we doubt? The disciples did. Instead of asking God to intervene and take care of things, they ask, "Do you care?"

You see, "fear does this. Fear corrodes our confidence in God's goodness. We begin to wonder if love lives in heaven. If God can sleep in our storms, if his eyes stay shut when our eyes grow wide, if he permits storms after we get on his boat, does he care? Fear unleashes a swarm of doubts...."[4] In Jesus's divine wisdom, he knew that fear would be one of the many things the human heart would contend with during life. Thus, he continually offered sheltering words, recorded in Scripture, such as, "Let not your hearts be troubled, neither let them be afraid" (John 14:27), and, "Fear not, little flock" (Luke 12:32).

In fear, we seem to muster enough courage to call out to God, but not enough to actually trust him. Don't get me wrong, turning to God in a storm is the right thing to do. In fact, it was something that Snow White failed to do in her late-night drama. However, we must not simply call, we must trust when we do, putting each and every storm in Christ's hands instead of keeping it in ours. Why? Because "perfect love casts out fear" (1 John 4:18), and this perfect love is Jesus Christ. Often, a spirit of abandonment or control might bog us down, and we feel like we must be the one to take the reins, believing that God won't or that he simply could not care less. This just is not true. God does care, and he will calm your each and every storm. He wants us to have faith, not fear. "For I, the Lord your God, / hold your right hand; / it is I who say to you, 'Fear not, / I will help you'" (Isaiah 41:13). You see, Jesus walks with us and is so close that he holds our *very hand*. Let us heed the voice of our late shepherd, Pope St. John Paul the Great, who often said, "Be not afraid." Collapse into Christ's arms instead of folding in on yourself like Snow White. We will find shelter in Jesus through prayer, meditating on Scripture, and by surrounding ourselves with close friends and family. If we do not, fear will certainly reign.

After facing an evening of adversity, Snow White's final response of the night is to crumble. If we let it, fear will paralyze us. However, in faith, we must dust ourselves off and follow Christ's command, "Rise, and have no fear" (Matthew 17:7). We all fall down sometimes, but when we do, even while under the weight of the cross, we must rise, knowing we are not alone. Of course disturbances will come, but the final outcome is contingent on what we do when the storm hits. If we let it, a drizzle can become a downpour of dread, doubt, and discouragement that pull us into despair and strip us of hope. This is just what the enemy wants to see. We must instead put our hope in Jesus.

Thus, "let us hold fast the confession of our hope, without wavering, for he who promised is faithful" (Hebrews 10:23). Don't let darkness and despair set up camp in your backyard. "Fear may fill our world, but it does not have to fill our hearts. It will always knock on the door… for heaven's sake don't offer it a bed for the night."⁵ The only fear you should hold in your heart is fear of the Lord.

Know that with every cross, a resurrection will come. Jesus said, "I am the resurrection and the life; he who believes in me, though he may die, yet shall he live" (John 11:25). In each storm we face, we may feel as though we have died, but in Christ we will be restored. Snow White's dungeon of fear fades away as the shadowy night disperses with the dawning of a new day—her resurrection, so to say. In the light of day, perspective is gained. We see a storm for what it really is, evaluate our own actions, and come to terms with why God allowed the storm to take place. In the case of Snow White, the surrounding eyes that once seemed scary are really the eyes of sweet animals. Perhaps we all imagine that our situations are worse than they are. Or, have you ever thought it possible that in those dark times, God's hand really is on you, sparing you from something more. You may wonder, "Why did God let that happen to me?" But, do you ever come out of a bad situation and think, *Wow, things could have been worse?* Maybe we are too focused on clutching yesterday's wild waves to see that indeed, when we called out, Jesus calmed the sea before it could clobber us.

In the end, Snow White comes to see that her fear was the true instigator of her dark night. In the brightness of morning, she has clarity and takes ownership of the storm, knowing that much of what she faced was a result of her fear. Thus, let the Lord's light shine upon you, and brighten your way for "the Lord (your) God lightens (your) darkness" (Psalm 18:28). Jesus does not want you to live in the depths of darkness. If you invite him into your storm, and ask him to fill the sails of your ship, he will free you and direct your way.

I encourage you to take a moment right now to call to mind and pray about what is plaguing you. "Is anyone among you suffering? Let him pray" (James 5:13). Do not be shy in turning to Christ. He is calling for you to come to him. Now, in prayer, invite Jesus to pull away the crust that has formed on your heart and reach in and restore your spiritual pulse, giving you life in him. Next, ask him to renew your trust in him and calm your storm. Ask Jesus to forgive you for any anger or resentment you have felt toward him. Repeat, "Jesus, have mercy on me. Jesus, I trust in you." In the coming days, continue to let go, and invite Jesus into your soul. Never forget the words of Christ, "In me you may have peace. In the world you have tribulation; but be of good cheer, I have overcome the world" (John 16:33).

In time, you will come to see your storms in a different way. Let them go. Open your heart to what is coming instead of what has occurred, and God will bring good out of your trials. Seek to learn from your thorny episode. After all, was it not through the bloody cross that Jesus brought life to the world? Jesus's mighty trial bore the sweetness of redemption. When Jesus was on the cross, he spoke the first verse of Psalm 22, "My God, my God, why hast thou forsaken me?" Jesus shares with us this very human response toward suffering, just as we share the cross with him when we suffer. "But rejoice in so far as you share Christ's suffering, that you may also rejoice and be glad when his glory is revealed" (1 Peter 4:13). We are invited to praise God, even in our times of suffering. In our own chapters of life, tribulation will come, but so will endurance, grace, and blessings.

Out of suffering, Snow White gained confidence. After joining in song with her forest friends, she declares that all will be well. We believe such an assertion from Snow White is possible because when it comes to fairy-tale kingdoms, we believe in a "happily ever after." In Christ's kingdom, we should believe in happy endings, too. God's promised goodness is not just reserved for those in heaven, but for those on earth, because the Church militant (that's us) is one with the Church triumphant (those in heaven). We are already living in the kingdom of heaven, so we do not have to wait for our final resurrection to receive heavenly blessings. Instead, we just have to open ourselves to what Christ is already offering to us, here and now.

After Snow White rises, she is ready to work toward turning her situation around. In all things we must pray, but we must also act. Turning to the woodland creatures, she inquires about a place to stay. The princess sees that the animals are well taken care of, and she hopes the same for herself. With some chirps and nods, they begin to guide her toward shelter. Therefore, not only do we need to be confident that Jesus will halt our hazards, but that he has a plan for every moment of our lives, our now. "For I know the plans I have for you, says the Lord, plans for welfare and not for evil, to give you a future and a hope" (Jeremiah 29:11).

Just like Snow White's chipmunk friends, who store seeds, berries, and nuts during those sunny spring and summer days, we must build up faith for our wintry moments and hold on to hope. Thus, when the tempest arrives, our heart will weather it, firm in the knowledge that Jesus has us covered. "Every one then who hears these words of mine and does them will be like a wise man who built his house upon the rock; and the rain fell, and the floods came, and the winds blew upon that house, but it did not fall, because it had been founded on the rock" (Matthew 7:24–25).

# Chapter Four

## WHISTLE WHILE YOU WORK
### ~ Threefold Vocation ~

Call it a rite of passage; I bought my first pair of work boots. I chose typical tan boots. However, I stripped the boots of the original brownish-yellow laces, opting instead to deck one boot out with hot pink and the other with neon green. I like to mix things up. Anyway, I was working as a youth director, and the annual WorkCamp week had arrived. WorkCamp is a week dedicated to improving homes in the local community—a week in which people work together in upholding the motto: "safer, drier, warmer." If anyone told me in high school, even college, that I would ever work in youth ministry, I would have laughed, but I guess God is the one who is laughing now. He knew what he was doing, knew my gifts, and would eventually lead me down this vocational path.

We all have our thoughts about what we will be doing when we grow up. For most of us, these predictions begin at an early age, mostly because adults tend to ask children that typical question: "What do you want to be when you grow up?" When I was asked, I would respond in dramatic fashion, saying, "I want to be a waitress and a star." At this point in my life, I can pat myself on the back for accomplishing one of those goals: I have been a waitress, though I am still working on the star part. But who isn't? It is normal for kids to come up with unique goals for themselves. Some of these ideas actually come to fruition in later years, while others become once-upon-a-time aspirations that we chuckle about in adulthood. Nonetheless, this idea of *purpose* is on our minds from a very young age: "Before doubt and accusation take hold, most little girls sense that they have a vital role to play; they want to believe there is something in them that is needed and needed desperately."[1] It is the call to mission. In the end, it is not just our notions that count, but also God's calling.

One of the many themes in *Snow White* is that of work. Throughout the story, we find Snow White joyfully working. She prompts her animal friends to whistle while they work. I don't know about you, but I don't just break into song randomly while completing a task. Rather, I have to be ushered by a sense of joy. All of us can learn an important lesson from Snow White's line of encouragement: We should be content in our work, doing something that will make us whistle. Untold hours of our lives will be dedicated to working, and we should put a lot of discernment into what kind of work we will do. The joy comes when we accept God's will for our lives and do the work to which we are called. Make no doubt about it; God is calling you or has called you to a purpose for his glory: "Each of us must discern, accept, and live out joyfully and generously the commitments, responsibilities, and roles to which God calls him or her."[2]

Just as Snow White looks to her animal acquaintances to help complete a task, God is looking to you to help him in his mission. Snow White assigns each creature a very specific duty to aid the restoration of the dwarfs' messy home. God wants us to tidy up our world by giving each of us a task, too. But, how do you know what exactly God is calling you to? Truly, the only way to know is to ask him in prayer, and then open your ears and heart to your divine assignment.

Sometimes, this means we have to remove ourselves from the noise around us and get away from our crazy, overscheduled lives. Maybe it's just time away from our screens and activities. For me, it took something bigger: I stepped away from the noise through travel. When I left to go to Ecuador, I didn't realize I had signed up for the discovery of both self and Christ. In reality, I just wanted to see the world, and going to South America seemed like a good way to further expand the small dent I had already made on the globe. Thoughts of seeing and treading on the mountains of Ecuador were enchanting. Amazing things happen on mountains. Thus, I call Ecuador my "mountaintop moment."

Have you ever noticed that in Scripture, some of the most amazing things happen in the wilderness? God tends to request an escape from the cityscape and orchestrates a new story in the wild when he has something important to teach and share. Many important scriptural events occurred on mountains. On Mount Ararat, Noah's ark came to rest after the flood. On Mount Sinai, Moses received the Ten Commandments. On Mount Carmel, the prophet Elijah challenged the false prophet Baal. In the New Testament, Jesus teaches his disciples on the Mount of Olives. He further reveals himself to Peter, James, and John the apostle in his Transfiguration, which occurs on Mount Tabor. And of course Jesus is crucified on Calvary, a mountain. Your own mountain might be unnamed, but Jesus is going to take you there—and when he does, you will leave changed.

In my sierra of solitude, God gave me the desire to begin a relationship with him. Admittedly, it was in boredom that I first decided to pray because I didn't have the glamour of life to absorb me—just like the Israelites, who were called out of the hustle and bustle of Egypt into the desert. But God knew what he was doing. On that mountaintop, he stripped me of all my distractions until I could no longer avoid his gaze. He was directing my view to the heavens. In my new prayerfully profound relationship with Jesus, I became invested in asking questions. I would ask, he would answer. No longer did I see God as distant. Instead, it was the first time that I clearly saw that God cared and prayer worked.

Then, it happened. I dared to ask God the question that is on every young adult's mind with great intensity: What am I called to do with my life? For two months straight, I prayed a vocational prayer daily through St. Joseph. And, after such an extended time of prayer with no answer, my newfound conviction and trust faltered. I stopped praying the vocational prayer, instead saying to myself: "This isn't working."

Now, it is important to note that God works in his timing, not ours. Therefore, perseverance is key. He does answer. He promised he would: "Ask, and it will be given you; seek, and you will find; knock, and it will be opened to you. For every one who asks receives, and he who seeks finds, and to him who knocks it will be opened" (Matthew 7:7–8). And so, in Jesus's divine timing, my answer came. When it did, I smirked. This has become my practice when I know Jesus has just shared the answer I have been longing for through prayerful persistence. If you don't already know the way God speaks to you, time and the practice of prayer will further reveal it. Begin simply by asking the questions that linger in your heart. He is always there waiting; we just have to dare to ask. It was when I asked—and listened for the Lord's answer—that my journey in youth ministry began.

So one long vacation revealed my vocation. But do we even understand what that means? One book I read claimed, "There is a widespread failure by Catholics to seek, discern, accept, and live out their personal vocations. To a considerable extent it comes from failure to realize that there is such a thing as personal vocation."[3] In the few times I heard the word *vocation* during high school, it seemed isolated to those moments after Mass when a priest would ask, "Do you have a vocation?" Back then I thought you only had a vocation if God was calling you to be a religious sister. But everyone has a vocation. And, filled with great beauty, your vocation will ultimately fill you with peace, not trepidation. So next time someone asks you if you have a vocation, you can confidently say, "Yes, I do."

Coming to understand what a vocation is will help you figure out what God is calling you to become. Overall, there are three parts of every Christian's vocation. At the very core of who you are is your *primary vocation*: being a baptized believer and follower of Jesus Christ. In other words, it is the universal call to holiness. "Thus, this is the calling to love God, love neighbor, do one's part to bring about the kingdom of God, and participate in the mission of the Church, which is Jesus's primary means for continuing his redemptive activity throughout history."[4] This first part of your vocation should affect the other choices you make in your life, and will influence the other two parts of your vocation. What we do, we should do as Christians. Does the world recognize our footprint?

The next step is to discover your personal vocation. This is the part of your vocation that is your career or job. Ultimately, your job should be something you are passionate about, something you are really good at that makes you come alive. Maybe it is playing the flute, playing soccer, singing, painting, horseback riding, counseling friends, first aid training, babysitting, cooking, or doing math equations. In fact, I'll bet you have a great many skills, talents, and desires within you. No doubt you also have dreams and aspirations. These things are unique to you, placed on your heart by the Creator himself. And the Church cannot wait to see how these talents of yours take shape.

For most people, the white cinderblock and often windowless walls of unnaturally lit classrooms, loads of homework, and exhausting routine are not the best for encouraging authentic passion. As a result, consider taking a class that is not in your normal sphere of interest, shadowing a neighbor at work, doing volunteer work (outside of a requirement or club resume), spending time hearing your grandparents' stories (and actually listening), signing up for and attending career day, getting a summer job, hosting a foreign exchange student, taking a mission trip, visiting a farm, studying abroad (perhaps Ecuador?), or taking on a semester internship. Do things that expand your vision of what is out there. Avoid being guided by technology alone or the latest trend of popular television shows. Besides, they always make jobs appear more interesting and glamorous than they really are. Nothing beats real experience or hearing real employees' actual opinions when you are discerning a career path—and these experiences can aid in the discovery of what you were made to do. Ultimately, "whoever regards [her]work as a mere source of income or as a pastime will perform it differently from the person who feels that [her] profession is an authentic vocation."[5]

Whatever personal vocation you pursue, you must make sure it is not in conflict with your primary vocation, which is living as a Christian. Thus, you must not yield to the world in the way you live out your vocation. Instead, you must live with a Christian standard and live out Church teaching. Maybe you will be a nurse, a teacher, or a missionary. Maybe you will follow the path to become a photographer, journalist, forensic scientist, or architect. The options are endless, but God is not calling us to blindly select something. He is asking us to come to his throne in prayer and discover all that we were meant to be and do for him. Your choice is important because personal vocation is "the unique, unrepeatable role God calls each baptized person to play in carrying out the all-embracing divine plan."[6]

The last part of your three-fold vocation is your *state of life*. This permanent commitment will determine further how you live out your primary and personal vocations. As a woman, your possible states of life include marriage, becoming a consecrated single, or becoming a religious sister/nun. God has a call just for you. Your state of life will not erase the desires of your heart or mission that you feel God has placed on your heart. Instead, it will help you to fulfill it. (Stay tuned for more on this in chapter fourteen.)

Keep in mind that all aspects of your vocation are not randomly received and "people do not give themselves personal vocations; these callings come from God."[7] Certainly, this idea of seeking what God wants over what we want would be rejected by the culture. Worldly ways are caught up in finding the job that will give you the most the biggest salary, the most recognition, and the highest degree of gratification. However, we will truly be happiest when we spend our lives doing what God made us to do. Do you trust that God's plan for your life will truly make you happy?

When I finally kneeled to our Lord, I found my calling. So often we keep our faith in a box, yet "faith ought to be—the basic principle organizing and integrating every Christian life."[8] We were made for Christ, and he has a very specific purpose for our lives. It is only in approaching and maintaining a relationship with Jesus through prayer and worship that we truly find our mission. Like the seven dwarfs, you may have to "dig, dig, dig," deep into yourself, through experiences, and in prayer to figure out your three-fold vocation. When you do, in Jesus's perfect timing, each layer of your vocation (primary, personal, and state of life) will be revealed to you—and every element will be connected.

As you live out the many aspects of your vocation, you will wear a lot of shoes—anything from high heels to work boots. You will weather work differently than a guy because women, in their bodies and in their lives, encounter seasons. (In chapter fifteen, you will see how this can shape your life). In the meantime, make it your pastime to find a purposeful pair of shoes to wear. In no time, you too will be saying, "It's off to work I go."

# Chapter Five

## WHO HAS BEEN USING MY FORK?
### ~ *Cohabitation* ~

As you are reading this, what if you were suddenly to hear a voice shout, "Fire!"? Most likely, such a word, said with such volume, would jolt you into action. As kids, the common phrase we learned was, "Stop, drop, and roll!" Whatever you'd do, it would be done solely to get out. No one wants to go down in flames.

Thankfully, I have never been in a real fire. Nonetheless, I have participated in plenty of fire drills—often unplanned. At colleges around the country, there are those 3:00 A.M. moments when some student's hand gravitates toward the fire alarm and pulls down, releasing a mighty blast of sound that interrupts everyone's sleep or studies. Bitter students descend several flights of steps, greeting each other in grogginess while unintentionally modeling their pajamas.

And even if you thought that someone was probably just pranking, you were still required to get yourself out of bed and march outside. Why? Because the possibility of a real fire always existed. If you did not, the next person to wake you up would not be your mom, but the local fire marshal, and he would not be wearing pajamas or a smile. While in college, I heard of several students who attempted to out-sleep the law. One in particular hid in the closet. Maybe he just got lost looking for his robe. The things people will do to avoid following the law!

In general, living in a residence hall with roommates and hall mates is definitely an interesting experience. During an unexpected crack-of-dawn gathering, you see all sides of a person, sometimes more than you wish to view. In fact, I always thought living with someone before knowing them was a strange and challenging way to get to know a person. It is no surprise to hear that some pairings do not result in peace. Close quarters create all kinds of possibilities for agitation: "Who has been sitting in my chair? Who has been eating off my plate? Who has been taking some of my bread? Who has been using my fork?"[1]

Speaking of roommates, did you ever find it odd that this cute little lady name Snow White had seven little men as housemates? Somehow, "seven dwarfs" sounds more innocent than "seven men." But let's face the facts. Sounds a bit scandalous, huh? Is it time to pull the fire alarm? I think it is time to get to the bottom of what sounds like a sketchy living situation. Some may try to reason that she had no place to go, or that the rent was cheap. But really, does that make it OK?

Allow me to share some secondhand advice with you. One thing that my mom taught me when I was a girl was to see the seven emotions of the man I planned to marry. These root emotions include joy, anger, surprise, trust, grief, fear, and love. She thought that this would allow me to discern if it was a good idea to marry the man at hand—and not to find myself surprised by a vice of great intensity. Obviously, there is a lot to get to know about a person, and some things go beyond emotions. Do they snore when they snooze, or leave the toothpaste cap-less continually? Can you handle these quirks? How do you manage to figure out all the sides of a person before you marry him? Modern culture would say: Live with the person. It's such a typical practice that many of us are not shocked to find out that our next door neighbor is living with a man—or seven of them. Many popular movies and television programs showcase this as well, and we have begun to digest this scandalous and sinful act as normal. We cannot let the culture in motion steal our vision of virtue. Instead, we must declare truth in the way we live our lives.

With that said, let us review Snow White's living situation. Certainly, she learns a whole lot about these guys rather quickly. Right away, she knows they are messy and that they do not clean their house or dishes. I cannot even imagine what their bathroom looked like! Upon meeting them, she pegs each dwarf's name immediately, names that summarize them as persons. As you already know, there was Sneezy, Sleepy, Dopey, Doc, Happy, Bashful, and Grumpy. In reality, it is very possible for one person to carry all those same characteristics and emotions. It is a good practice to get to know someone, their many nicknames, moods, and modes, but the manner of acquiring such information must be considered.

So, was Snow White's living situation innocent or impure? Is this household about to go up in flames? Overall, what makes a living situation sweet or sour? Let's begin by reviewing the facts about cohabitation. First, what is cohabitation? Often it is masked and appears to be something other than it is, but we cannot dance around cohabitation's core connotation. Truthfully, it is when two people who are romantically involved reside in the same place. In other words, they are living together in a sexual relationship outside of marriage. We know from sacred Scripture that fornication is a sin (see Galatians 5:19). Such a living situation may mirror marriage, but it falls short without a vow to secure faithfulness. In a sense, it is a theater production titled *House*. Everyone plays a part, and there is always the lingering threat of being replaced by an understudy. When the curtain is drawn, a cohabiter may find himself or herself without a part and a partner. Because of this, no matter how popular the play, cohabitation is one production that the Church cannot applaud. Instead, Mother Church leaves the exit sign aglow, and prompts the use of a fire extinguisher.

Of course the threat of failure is known. So, that leads us to ask the question: Why do people still cohabitate? Motivation may come from a sense of convenience, whether for more time together or affordability. Others choose it for the sake of discernment because they do not want to make a marital mistake, and they hope that living with a person will help them know if they should tie the knot.[2] Some fear making a commitment or losing personal independence. Since it has become a cultural norm, many consider it to be the inevitable next step in a serious relationship. And other people settle on cohabitating because of impatience; they don't want to wait to engage in physical intimacy, so they trade lifetime love and authentic intimacy for the fleeting pleasure of the flesh.

Ultimately, people who cohabitate are seeking to safeguard themselves, but in reality they are setting themselves up for destruction. They seek to live separate lives yet become bonded in body and heart, but all with an uncommitted undercurrent. No one who enters into such a relationship will flee unscathed. Some of the reasons for this lifestyle may appear to be practical, but living together is immoral, and, statistically speaking, it turns out that those who cohabitate before marriage actually have a higher rate of divorce.[3] Overall, the divorce rate of cohabiting couples is about 80 percent, according to Bennett.[4] "Couples who cohabited prior to marriage have greater marital conflict and poorer communication, and they made more frequent visits to marriage counselors. Women who cohabited before marriage are more than three times as likely to cheat on their husbands within marriage. They were also more than three times as likely to be depressed as married women, and the couples were less sexually satisfied than those who waited for marriage."[5] Trust me—you won't be the exception.

If you want your relationship to last, it is better not to live together. Be honest, if you could have taste-tested your family, would you have stayed for the main meal? When things get tough in our families, thoughts of bailing may cross our minds. However, most of us know that, despite daily dramas, we would never follow through with a departure. There is a sense of great security found within the boundaries of blood. For the most part, we know that no quirky habit or mood will dissolve the kinship, so we are able to be ourselves: at our best and our worst. Who does not want this same sense of security with a spouse someday? Instead, seeing cohabitation as a trial period that can be halted at any time, often couples who live together before marriage duck tough issues, repress anger, and avoid criticism of each other's annoying behavior.[6] How could any of those actions and emotions breed permanence, faithfulness, or authentic love?

True discernment comes when we step back and seek God's ways and will. The purpose of a romantic relationship is unity, but cohabitation does not truly allow this. Instead, it is a forgery and a roadblock to true love. It is built on fear, doubt, false comfort, and convenience. It is a relationship of selfishness, not selflessness—a relationship without sacrifice or change. Despite what the culture declares, this isn't the fuel a relationship can run on. It is a dead-end road in this life and will not lead us to the everlasting life we were made for: God's love in heaven. Choose the right way. "Enter by the narrow gate; for the gate is wide and the way is easy, that leads to destruction and those who enter by it are many. For the gate is narrow, and the way is hard, that leads to life, and those who find it are few" (Matthew 7:13–14). Doing what is right can take a lot of work, but it is always the best way and the path to true fulfillment.

So we return to our snowy suspect and dubious dwarf defendants. Were they seven sinners, or practically siblings? I'd say the latter. First off, Snow White is very concerned with keeping things pure. On her arrival, she sweeps the house clean, and she demands that the dwarfs wash their hands before dinner. These acts are physical, but can remind us of the spiritual. As Catholics, we are always seeking to be made clean—through the use of water in baptism, at the fonts filled with holy water, and through penance. In the spirit of Snow White, keep your house, body, and soul clean by pursuing holy ways. As in the case of Grumpy, who revolts against getting washed, it is not always easy to purify habits, but it is necessary. And just like the dwarfs' drenching of Grumpy, sometimes being a good friend means prompting purity by way of a splash or fire hose. Overall, the dwarfs and Snow White know how to have good clean fun, from dining to dancing.

When it comes to sleeping arrangements, the seven men, in keeping with virtue, sacrifice their comfort and convenience to offer Snow White their bedroom, while they sleep in a separate quarter. Moreover, at the beginning of a new workday, Snow White keeps her affection holy with a simple and temperate kiss for each dwarf, just like a sister might kiss a little brother. And the way a brother protects his sister from danger is how these dwarfs seek to protect their adopted sister Snow White. Men must learn to protect women from fires, and women must learn to flee from flames. Otherwise, both will meet a fiery fate. Keep in mind, of course, that most men are not like the innocent dwarfs. You shouldn't be living with someone of the opposite sex, unless he is truly your brother or cousin.

So, let's review: The only time you should be seeing your Romeo's robe is outside during a public fire drill. If you are unmarried, you do not yet hold the pajama privilege, and you need to remove yourself from the threatening fire. It is time to evacuate! "He has placed before you fire and water: / stretch out your hand for whatever you wish. / Before a man are life and death / and whichever he choose will be given to him" (Sirach 15:16–17). Just like Adam and Eve, our mortal sins may cause us to hide away, whether it be behind a bush in the Garden of Eden or in our closet during a fire drill. Do not let yourself go down in the flames. Just like any faithful fireman, Jesus will find you. Allow yourself to be found—and willing to follow his exit plan. Cohabitation is not the key to joy, a saintly life, or true unity, but marriage can be.

# Chapter Six

## WOMEN ARE POISON
### ~ *Guys versus Girls* ~

Growing up with only brothers was certainly an interesting experience—a privilege at times, a challenge at others. My brothers intrigued me. Their ways were mysterious in comparison to my own. In our childhood years we journeyed jointly, and, still, that didn't help me understand them any better. Moreover, I never really grasped the possibility that my brothers' actions could be universal to all boys. For me, my dealings were isolated to them, thinking that was just how my brothers behaved toward me, their sister. I suppose we recognized our differences on some level. Maybe it's why they always made the sacrifice of carrying the weight of me on their back when we played ranch: I the rancher, my brothers the horses. Or why they felt the need to team up and pelt me from the top of their bunk bed with pillows—perfect bombs for a target half their size. Or why they told me that if I did not start eating more at dinner that I would turn into a dot on a page, and they would erase me. How could I forget those days?

Why did I put up with such ridiculous tactics and boyish schemes? Well, all the days of my childhood, my two older brothers had convinced me that they had a club, one that I was not privy to as the little sister. But oh, how I wanted to be accepted into the club. I wanted to share in the secrets and camaraderie; so much so, that the instant I was ready to snitch to mom, they would declare that I would not be a part of the club if I did. In hopes of making the cut, I never tattled. My brothers knew what they were doing. Turns out, of course, there never really was an official club. All the nicknames I endured, such as "Ping" and "Dog Nose," all those trips with me in the middle car seat as my brothers played live Ping-Pong with my head done in vain.

However, as I grew up, I realized that guys really do have a club, unofficial in title as it may be. Male members meet in moments on the basketball court, in the locker room, seated in sports stadiums, on camping trips and hikes into the wilderness, over pizza, or at car shows. Men gather to bond and beat their chests. No matter how hard a girl tries and desires this, she will never be a part of the boys' club. Why? Because girls' chests are not flat, and beating them just isn't one of our hobbies. Clearly, on the physical level, we recognize that men and women are different. This seems to be obvious to everyone. Yet, secular culture tries to purposefully forget these differences.

Awareness of this difference between guys and girls comes at an early age. Most classes from pre-K to eighth grade have a rift down the center, where boys sit on one side and girls sit on the other. For the most part in class, girls and boys do not dare to mix or mingle. In those childhood and young adolescent chapters, boys roll around in dirt and play war, making weapons out of rubber bands. While girls make hot chocolate out of that same dirt, put it in teacups, and use rubber bands to secure ponytails and braids at their mobile hair salons. Despite years of war games, boys cannot seem to break the girls' code. Thus, boys remain baffled, but certainly intrigued, by females. The same is true for girls. Even with many conversations over muddy tea about guys, girls continue to find boys much of a mystery.

Soon enough, boys become young men, and girls become young women. Nevertheless, differences only seem more present in the new heights and shapes of both genders. However, there is a greater boldness, as boys brave talking to ladies, and girls catch moments away from their female friends to enjoy time with young men in school hallways. It is in those conversations and interactions that both begin to realize that the differences between men and women are not just surface and skin. Instead, males and females are innately different, and this affects everything: interests, behavior, speech, and emotions. Yet again, this is something our culture tries to play down.

The best thing we can do is learn what truly makes men and women who they are—and how these truths shape each gender group. Let's not be grumpy about our differences like Grumpy, who had a negative notion and skewed sense about women. We see this when he first meets Snow White, saying with disapproval "All females is poison!"[1] Instead, we must learn to accept differences and allow this recognition to form our understanding and guide our interactions with the opposite sex. Acknowledging the differences between the sexes will also allow women to be who they were made to be and strive to be women, not men.

Thus, first it is important to understand yourself as a woman. Are women poison or poised? Woman's truest identity lends itself to the latter. Individually, you, as a person, are a unique creature of God; therefore, no one like you has ever been created nor will anyone like you ever be fashioned again. With that said, you are also a woman, and this molds you as a person. "Whatever it means to bear God's image, you do so *as a woman*. That's how and where you bear his image."[2] In your femininity, your heart has been written with certain desires and needs, hopes and dreams. The beginning pages of this book speak about the reality of a royal chamber in the halls of the heart that store thoughts of princesshood. What more is stowed away within the depths of woman?

Perhaps at her core, a woman needs to feel profoundly loved on a variety of levels through an array of behaviors. Such love needs to be expressed often through constant action—words and deeds that appeal to her heart. "If she doesn't feel loved, it's the same for her as if she isn't loved."[3] But a woman's heart yearns for more than the rescue; she wants a romance that's continual. "A little girl longs for romance, to be seen and desired, to be sought after and fought for."[4] This desire is universal to toddler, tween, teen, maid, and matron. A lady should find this love first in God, her family, and friends. In God's timing, the prince called to love her will be revealed.

Within the context of love, a young woman wants to feel protected in multiple ways: emotionally, physically, and financially. Yes, there's a damsel in all of us, and we want men who are both capable and willing to slay dragons, even if the biggest dragon that ever rears its ugly head is a bad day, a mean teacher, or difficult boss. "We long for the protection masculine strength offers. To have them shield us from physical harm, yes. But also to have them shield us from emotional harm and spiritual attack."[5] Ladies should look to their father first to supply such strength, and, beyond earthly fathers, we can rely most on God the Father. His strength abounds, and he is ready to offer it to his daughters! In time, a woman should look for the same quality in the man that will become her husband.

Out of all the ways to feel secure, most women desire to be emotionally secure.[6] Thus, it is not cash flow but care-filled moments that matter most to ladies. A gal will feel emotionally secure through assuring gestures, the investment in quality time, and when she feels heard and understood. Often, when a young woman is sorting through an issue, she simply needs to speak her mind, and not have a guy try to fix it. In stormy moments, ladies do not want guys to offer solutions, but are simply looking to share their story and get feedback that confirms that they have been heard. Tell the guys in your life that some affirming words, nods, and even a hug are the types of things a woman desires when she is sharing something that is weighing on her.

If those first two components—love and protection—are the keys to a lady's heart, then what else is stored within? An important part of women's nature is that we are relational beings: Women are daughters, sisters, wives, mothers, and in all that friends. Ladies love to spend time with others and to care for the people in their lives. In fact, from the very beginning women have been relational. When Eve arrived, Adam already *was*. He had some time to hang out on his own, yet Eve's first breath sang in unison with his; she was born into relationship. Moreover, Eve was made in a relational way because God used Adam's body to bring her into existence. From a man's rib Eve arrived, whereas God formed Adam out of dust (Genesis 2).

"Female interests are centered on the human side of their lives: their family life, their relationships to those they love, their concern about their health, their welfare and, if they are Christians, the spiritual welfare of their children's souls; in other words, about human concerns. Most men speak about the stock market, politics, and sports; some speak about intellectual and artistic questions."[7] This distinction of interests can often be seen in conversation between genders. Girls like to talk about things directly involving or affecting people, and guys are drawn to speaking about *stuff*.

Undeniably, stamped in the depths of woman is this relational makeup. This reality can even be seen in her body. One of the greatest expressions of this relational identity is that a woman's body has been molded and prepared for the capacity to carry within her another human being. It is woman, not man, who has the ability to bear children. In *Mulieris Dignitatem*, St. John Paul II wrote, "Scientific analysis fully confirms that the very physical constitution of women is naturally disposed to motherhood—conception, pregnancy and giving birth—which is a consequence of the marriage union with the man."[8] Thus, what goes on within her body has an impact on who she is as an individual. Women are relational to the core.

Despite popular culture's doubts, men are in fact different from women. "God doesn't make generic people; he makes something very distinct—a man or a woman. In other words, there is a masculine heart and a feminine heart, which in their own ways reflect or portray to the world God's heart."[9] Perhaps, it is time to dissect the mechanical workings of the male mind. As you explore the compartments of the heart of man, you may begin to see how he *complements* you as a woman.

To begin, unlike ladies, guys have a greater call to feel respected than loved. Actually, giving a man respect is what makes him feel loved and trusted.[10] What exactly does respecting a man look like in concrete ways? When it comes to affirmation, a woman needs to hear those three short words of "I love you." Yet, for a man, the words "I respect you" just don't do it—actions speak louder than words. In particular, a man yearns for a woman to respect his judgment and decisions. Also, men have a need for a lady to respect their abilities. Women need their beauty affirmed, while men desire acknowledgment of their skills in both actions and words. Each woman has the power to build up or tear down the man closest to her, such as her father or fiancé, with her words. File this info away for the start of your marital union.

Each woman has a desire to have a man provide for her. Interestingly, this coincides with how a man is wired. Shaunti Feldhahn writes in her book *For Women Only*, "We have all heard that men want to be providers. They want to club the buffalo over the head and drag it to the cave to their woman. But what few women understand is that this is not just an issue of 'wanting to.' Rather, it is a burden that presses heavily on them and won't let up."[11] This is universal to all men, no matter the age or race. Though it is an unproven theological theory, I find it fascinating that women are so relational and that the root that sprung them into existence, through God, was a human bone; while Adam came from the dusty earth, and now he is drawn to work the same soil from which he emerged in order to provide. In comparison, women prefer to put their energy into others. Both sexes are driven by their beginnings.

Another important thing for young women to grasp about guys is that they are visual creatures. In a way, this is a very good thing in regard to a woman's desire to capture the eye of her beloved—he has a gaze for beauty. However, this means something a bit different than what a gal might understand "visual" to mean. For instance, most guys do not notice a lady's added accessories, such as the studs in her ears or shoes on her feet, but rather her built-in accessories, such as her bust or behind. Thus, how a woman frames her features will have a direct impact on the visual knowledge a man immediately receives by glancing at her. (More on the importance of flattering, but not flaunting, fashion in chapter nine.)

Very briefly, it is important to address why these differences exist between men and women. One important reason is that "the sexes are different because their brains are different. The brain, the chief administrative and emotional organ of life, is differently constructed in men and in women; it processes information in a different way, which results in different perceptions, priorities and behaviour."[12] For years, the concept of nature versus nurture has been debated. The ideas of social conditioning, parental expectations, and predetermined gender views certainly come into play, but what if I also told you that differences are detected as early as in the womb?

These days, many couples choose to find out the sex of their baby through the use of technology during the pregnancy. Yet, the body part below the belt is not the only gender-specific organ that shows a baby to be either male or female. Male or female hormones will shape the body, as well as the brain. Therefore, the brain also becomes sexed as male or female in the womb.[13] "How the brain circuitry is arranged affects more than our sexual inclination. It will make us, male or female, tend toward different attitudes, responses, feelings about ourselves and others, priorities…all the hundreds of differences noted throughout the ages by poets, writers, and ordinary men and women, in blissful scientific ignorance."[14]

Finally, on a spiritual level, it is essential to know that your soul is also different as a female. As the *Catechism* teaches, "Sexuality affects all aspects of the human person in the unity of his body and soul" (*CCC* 2332). Thus, since you are a woman, your soul also has a female identity. Moreover, "the connection between body and emotion sheds light on the deep link existing between a man's body and his soul."[15] Anyone can acknowledge that emotional sadness can affect your body. You don't want to get out of bed because you are down, or when you might feel that you are not beautiful when you are sick. Humans are composite beings made up of body and soul, and both make us who we are. A "woman's soul is present and lives more intensely in all parts of the body; and it is inwardly affected by that which happens to the body."[16] Perhaps this idea can be most profoundly seen in pregnancy, which happens in the body while very much influencing the soul. Our differences are down to the soul, and without a doubt that's a good thing!

The Church acknowledges that the sexes are physically, morally, and spiritually different. The beauty that she points out is that these differences unite men and women. There is a complementarity between both (see *CCC* 2333), like two puzzle pieces that are able to come together because of a harmonizing shape. This, of course, is fully revealed in marriage and family life. Therefore, men and women should be content—even ecstatic—in their differences, seeing their unique composition as a way that unites rather tears apart. It allows for a beautiful partnership.

In reading this, you know that being a woman is much more complex than is described here. In the same way, there is a lot more to men. This chapter is only the beginning—yet important, nevertheless, in raising an awareness that, indeed, men and women are different. Acknowledging our differences will help us to be more authentic women in all areas and relationships of our lives, always seeking to be full of poise, not poison. It will also help us to be secure in who we are, instead of striving to be something we are not—men. In no way do differences elevate one sex over the other. The dignity of men and women is equal (see *CCC* 2334). Therefore, "everyone, man and woman, should acknowledge and accept his sexual identity" (*CCC* 2333). God ordained you to be woman, and in that he has a plan for you to live that out. For that reason, "live a life worthy of the calling to which you have been called" (Ephesians 4:1). You'll be a lot happier for it!

# Chapter Seven

## WHOEVER ATE A PIECE OF IT WOULD SURELY DIE

### ~ Sin and Temptation ~

"Welcome to paradise!" These words greeted us when our small boat's engine rumbled to a halt, and we drifted into the petite harbor of Isabela Island. For some, Isabela is a mere dot on the map, a forgotten treasure within the Galapagos archipelago. Stepping upon the sandy shoreline felt novel. The Australian and his kiwi[1] wife, who had been passengers on the same boat, announced that this particular island was off the beaten path. It seemed that the two rugged travelers thrived off of finding secret gems that most tourists had not yet discovered.

Admittedly, I too felt a bit special to visually drink in something so few had seen. For certain, this land felt rather unexplored, containing a sheltered beauty. The air was salty, the water was an enchanting color of blue, and the setting sun saturated the sky with the intensity of a firecracker, glowing a vibrant pink. The animal species were numerous and unique to my normal animal encounters: waved albatrosses, marine iguanas, sea lions, spotted eagle rays, the massive Galapagos tortoise, penguins, sharks, dolphins, crabs, a countless variety of finches, the red-billed tropic bird, flamingos, and more.

In the end, the appellation of paradise proved to be quite fitting. One morning, as I headed to the beach, I came across an apple tree, which was equipped with a sign that warned that the apples growing from it were poisonous to humans. After coming across such a sign, I remember cynically thinking, "Maybe this really *is* paradise?" Without a doubt, I was amused to be faced with a real poisonous apple tree. Deadly apples were only things from Scripture's description of the Garden of Eden or in fairy tales—or, were they? Perhaps, all of us encounter more toxic produce that we think. Anyhow, who would be silly enough to eat a poisonous apple when the secret is out by way of a hanging sign?

Just through east coast living, I have become a bit of an apple connoisseur. Autumn is filled with everything apple: apple pie, apple butter, apple cider, applesauce, and one of my favorites, caramel apples. Have you ever made caramel apples? They are delicious, and they look beautiful too! You know the process: Take your choice apple, put a stick in it, dip it in that creamy warm liquid called caramel, and finish it off by dressing it with an array of toppings, such as coconut, crushed Oreos, chocolate sprinkles, and marshmallows. I'll bet just hearing about it makes you want one right now! Isn't that just how temptation works? In reality, every woman's apple of temptation is dressed differently.

Let us pull back paradise's botanical curtain and once again reflect on original temptation and sin. Remember the serpent's cunning script?

> Now the serpent was more subtle than any other wild creature that the Lord God had made. He said to the woman, "Did God say, 'You shall not eat of any tree of the garden'?" And the woman said to the serpent, "We may eat of any fruit of the trees of the garden; but God said, 'You shall not eat of the fruit of the tree which is in the midst of the garden, neither shall you touch it, lest you die.'" But the serpent said to the woman,

"You will not die. For God knows that when you eat of it your eyes will be opened and you will be like God, knowing good and evil." So when the woman saw the tree was good for food, and that it was a delight to the eyes, and the tree was to be desired to make one wise, she took of its fruit and ate; and she also gave some to her husband, and he ate. (Genesis 3:1–6).

Face it: Satan made things look pretty appealing. He played the mind games, he lied, and he managed to convince Eve that God was holding out on her, all by dressing sin in a disguise. Some may say it looked as pretty as a caramel apple.

This same costumed apple exists in fairy tales, as well. In *Snow White and the Seven Dwarfs*, we get the benefit of seeing behind the scenes, peering into the enemy's pome preparation—a rather dramatic process beginning with a bubbling hot cauldron of liquid that is far from the innocence of golden caramel. A dainty, dangling apple is placed in the poisonous potion, and the curse is spoken by the cunning queen. When the apple emerges, blue goo drips from it, and we get a glimpse of the reality that is now set within it, seeing the face of death upon it. "The apple was so cunningly made."[2] The queen knows that anything that looks like death is not appealing. So, with some final words, the apple's toxic truth is masked. "Outside it looked pretty, white with a red cheek, so that everyone who saw it longed for it; but whoever ate a piece of it would surely die."[3]

Undoubtedly, sin and temptation often have a very attractive appearance. If they didn't, no one would struggle with them. Moreover, sin holds empty promises, which is usually the thing that makes us desire a bite. We are convinced (even just subconsciously) that when we enter into a sin, it will be the answer to a need or desire. Also, sin is taking something that was once a good and twisting it; that's all Satan can do. He steals; he does not create—he's just not that powerful.

Protect yourselves from moments of temptation by forming your conscience so you can determine if an action is right or wrong—seeking to act on true knowledge instead of acting in the moment, or on emotion. "Moral conscience, present at the heart of the person, enjoins him at an appropriate moment to do good and to avoid evil. It also judges particular choices, approving those that are good and denouncing those that are evil" (*CCC* 1777). Our freedom is found not in eating tainted grub, but by freely choosing what is good and of God. "Man has the right to act in conscience and in freedom so as personally to make moral decisions" (*CCC* 1782). God doesn't force us to do good, even if it is best for us. This is where our free will comes in; we must *choose* the good.

In Eden, God had told Adam and Eve not to eat of the tree of knowledge of good and evil. However, God also said, "neither shall you touch it, lest you die" (Genesis 3:3). How interesting that God warns our first parents *not* to eat the fruit, but also not to even *touch* it. In this context, touching something is like putting yourself in the near occasion of sin, a place or situation in which you will be tempted to do what is wrong. Thus, to touch is to enter into temptation, and to taste is to indulge in an offense against God. When God said that man and woman would die, he was not speaking primarily of a physical death. Instead, Our Lord was referencing a spiritual death—death of our souls.

In *Snow White*, eating the edible ruby would lead the princess to be buried alive. In the same way, after modern woman sins, she can still walk and breathe, but she has just cut herself off from God, Creator of all. "Mortal sin…turns man away from God, who is his ultimate end and his beatitude, by preferring an inferior good to him" (*CCC* 1855).

Without God, there is no life. Therefore, mortal sin is like being buried alive. "For the wages of sin is death" (Romans 6:23).

Can you imagine falling asleep and then awakening in a dark and snug space, which you soon realize is your coffin? Heavy dirt keeps your death box in the ground. You scream and scratch the tight boundaries around you, but no one can hear you. No one would deny that the mere thought of being buried alive is horrifying; and yet, it happens every time we enter into grave sin (pun intended). No matter how glamorous the world attempts to make death's casket of sin, in reality, unlike Snow White's tomb, ours won't be clad in glass and gold. In living a life with unrepented sin, "you are like whitewashed tombs, which outwardly appear beautiful, but inside are full of dead men's bones and all uncleanness" (Matthew 23:27).

As discussed, every woman's apple is dressed distinctively because every woman has her own temptations and motivations for taking a bite. Let's look at the step-by-step play between the witch and the princess. First, it is important to note that, like many women, Snow White has a *desire* written on her heart, one for a prince. Just a little while ago, she was publicly professing her feelings for Prince Ferdinand to her seven hosts. Thus, when the witch comes in contact with Snow White, she plays on this longing.

Second, the witch's first contact with Snow White is done with great *intimidation*. Snow White is baking in the kitchen, singing more notes about her prince, when the witch appears out of nowhere, casting a shadow upon the cottage and startling the young woman. Knowing the little men would be away, she seeks to put an end to Snow White. This parallels Eve's experience with the enemy, as both women were intimidated when found solo. Yes, we often hear Satan described as a snake, and if you are like me, you're not much of a fan of those slithery creatures. However, it is important to point out that the Hebrew word for snake is *nahash*, which translates to "sea monster." Sounds even more intimidating than a mere serpent, doesn't it? Therefore, the creature Eve came across probably panicked her. This was no small threat.

Third, another slimy tactic of the enemy is to *plant doubt* in its victim. Before Snow White's run-in with the wrinkled woman, she was content in the kitchen, where she stood making gooseberry pie. However, upon her entrance the adversary declares that men crave apple pie over gooseberry. Suddenly, Snow White begins to question her initial choice—and we are no different from the protagonist in this fairy tale. We all doubt. This doubt can be about a variety of things: our looks, our personality, our abilities, our future, our choices, and so on. With doubt burrowed within, it can be easy to follow the trends and seek to blend in. Why make gooseberry pie when apple pie is what is popular?

If it were not for Snow White's flock of furry and feathery friends, danger would have engulfed her immediately. Unlike the princess turned prey, the creatures know that what is being offered to her is no good. Has this ever happened to you? Have you had someone in your life trying to tell you that something is not good? Maybe it is a choice you are making about an action, an entertainment selection, a situation you have placed yourself in, or a person in your life. Yet so often, when someone expresses distaste, we don't think they know what they are talking about. Maybe these voices in our lives are worth considering.

Clearly, Snow White doubts the validity of the animals' concern. As they swarm the weathered witch, Snow White waves them off and tells them to stop frightening an old lady. Little does Snow White realize that the enemy wears a façade in order to draw her into tasting the apple at hand. When we ignore wisdom—from a parent, friend, teacher, youth minister, priest, or Church teaching—we just might be setting ourselves up for a hazardous plunge. There is great value in learning from what others have gleaned from their personal experiences, all their ups and downs. In this instance, we can all learn from Snow White.

Using trickery, the witch fakes heart problems. The devil will do whatever it takes to invade your home and soul. Snow White takes the bait and brings death right into the cottage. Do we sometimes welcome evil into our lives without knowing? Because evil is often masked in a disguise, we have to be particularly discerning and objective about this.

Once the witch is inside the residence, her deception continues, as she tells Snow White she has a secret to share. Of course, the devil's legions know that man is *stirred by curiosity*. Holding out the blood red fruit, the enemy shares that the apple is magical, and with one bite, dreams become realities. The princess is filled with amazement and responds, "Really?"

Seeing an opening, an unspoken desire on Snow White's heart, the queen queries her about her desires and love interest. When Snow White admits that she is in love, the queen is finally able to place the apple of desire into the hands of her target. "Snow White longed for the apple."[4] It is desire that finally induces Snow White, who was hoping for her dreams to be instantly fulfilled. Like the princess, no one likes to wait. Yet, God's timing is perfect: "For still the vision awaits its time; / it hastens to the end—it will not lie. / If it seems slow, wait for it; / it will surely come, it will not delay" (Habakkuk 2:3). We must trust the Lord, his timing and his plan instead of taking the apple into our hands.

Satan can only offer us despair. He plays on our impatience, twists our desires, and feeds us a fatal reality. The enemy's faulty promises yield only death. Upon Snow White's declaration of her dream and a simple bite, she instantly feels strange and dies. In gloomy victory, the witch rejoices with a cackle. The sky opens and it rains, as if heaven cries for the loss. Upon Snow White's death, the witch once again looks upon her mirror. "It answers at last, 'Oh, Queen, in this land you are the fairest of them all.' Then her envious heart had rest, so far as an envious heart can have rest."[5]

Lucifer, who was known as the most beautiful angel, fell due to his pride and vanity. In envy, Satan continues to attack God's most beautiful creation, woman, all in hopes of snatching her beauty for his own false glory. For the devil "was angry with the woman, and went off to make war on the rest of her offspring, on those who keep the commandments of God and bear testimony to Jesus" (Revelation 12:17). Thus, you must be vigilant. "Be sober, be watchful…[and] resist him, firm in your faith" (1 Peter 5:8–9).

Discerning what apples to eat and not eat is important. Start now. The witch set out to close Snow White's eyes forever through death. We have already discussed that death is the result of sin; we are the devil's victims. Perhaps there is something further to understand about eyes being closed. Yes, Snow White's eyes closed when an instantaneous sleeping death consumed her, but there is more. In our choices, our eyes can be closed. The more we choose to eat bad apples, the more we may no longer even see that what we are consuming is bad. Discernment gets dumped. Sin leaves us morally blind. Don't be blind to your sins, and don't linger in denial that your bad apples do you no harm.

So here is my question to you: What are your bad apples? Again, every woman's apple is dressed differently. What are your dreams and desires? Do you trust God to fulfill them? Or have you left God out of your decisions and taken matters into your own hands? Have you welcomed evil into your life? What have you eaten lately?

There are a couple of key areas in life that can be bad apples for ladies, and the first is guys. If a girl settles on someone just to feel loved and affirmed, a boy becomes a bad apple. Maybe a woman pursues a guy instead of letting go and waiting for him to do the pursuing. Maybe she does not preserve herself for her husband (see Proverbs 31:10–11), but acts unchaste. (For more on authentic love and tools to help you stay pure, see chapter twelve.)

Just like Snow White, surely there have been times when you have welcomed evil into your life. Everything looks innocent, and, despite advice to avoid certain things, we think we know best. We wave our friends, family, or mentors off when we watch secular shows, attend movies laced with immorality, spend time in bad company (see 1 Corinthians 15:33), listen to music that is lyrically lined with lies and seduction, and read trendy books that are teaching anything but Christian concepts. I am not saying all TV shows, movies, music, and books are bad, but I am saying that discernment should lead you to avoid many of them.

Every Christian needs to filter what they are absorbing. With the Christian call come certain obligations. "As obedient children, do not be conformed to the passions of your former ignorance, but as he who called you is holy, be holy yourselves in all your conduct" (1 Peter 1:14–15). These entertaining apples look appealing, but what is behind that waxy skin? What message is being shared or broadcasted, and from what source does it originate? If Christians digest pagan culture, they will be guided and shaped in pagan thought. Honestly, watching pagan shows and just ignoring the bad parts is not the way to sanctity. You have probably heard that phrase: "You are what you eat." Remember that. "Do you not know that friendship with the world is enmity with God?" (James 4:4). Instead of emulating what is popular by the world's standards, be a trendsetter and dare to be different for Christ. He has better things for you than what the world is offering. Bake gooseberry pie every once in awhile instead of the oh-so-popular apple. That's what Snow White set out to do originally. Stand true!

Another good question to ask yourself is, "What do I feed others?" Just like Eve, who after indulging in the fruit of sin, "also gave some to her husband, and he ate" (Genesis 3:6), ladies offer others bad apples when they gossip about others. Gossip is anything that harms someone's reputation or will cause emotional pain. We should not be seeking to get a rise out of someone else's misfortune or life's turbulence. "Let no evil talk come out of your mouths, but only such as is good for edifying, as fits the occasion, that it may impart grace to those who hear" (Ephesians 4:29). Seek to build up, not tear down, others.

Another bad apple offering is mood swings. A negative attitude or abrasive emotions are horrible things to dispense to others, especially when dealing with those that we love most. No one deserves to be treated harshly or poorly, and we should offer our best side to the people in our lives. Moodiness should never be justified. No matter what, God's daughters are called to charity. Finally, we should avoid spilling bad words. Such words sully us and those around us. "What comes out of the mouth proceeds from the heart, and this defiles a man" (Matthew 15:18).

Sin will often look good; it is a battle, and it is not always easy to say no by avoiding a bite of whatever is before you. However, it is very important to question what you are being fed, as well as what the source is. Is the supply coming from the secular world and Satan, or does it stem from the Church and God? In the end, if we keep eating bad apples, our souls will die. God is feeding us truth and life and says to each of us, "Keep my commandments and live, / keep my teachings as the *apple of your eye*; / bind them on your fingers, / write them on the tablet of your heart" (Proverbs 7:2–3, emphasis added). God our Father wants our gaze to be on the good, not the bad apples. Thus, we must not just know God's truths; we must be attentive to the commandments, desire the truth, and strive to live by those standards. His truths must shape our reality—our actions, our thoughts, and our very selves. Sadly, we can know something is wrong and still choose to do it. Living for Christ in every moment is always a choice, a choice to eat the bad apple, or leave it behind.

In those moments of weakness when we commit sin, we must not hide, as Adam and Eve did after sinning (see Genesis 3:8), but face our Creator. He is our redemptive remedy. Jesus's gift to us is the forgiveness of sins through the sacrament of confession, won for us through his sacrifice on Calvary (see John 20:19–23). Funny enough, the last time I went into a confessional, I found myself pondering how I felt like I was in an upright casket. And, fittingly, each and every time I tell all that I have done, upon absolution, I am made new. When I exit that tomb, I experience a spiritual resurrection. Forget Prince Ferdinand—Christ is the real prince that awakens your soul from the coffin through the sacraments and prayer. "You were buried with him in baptism, in which you were also raised with him through faith…and you, who were dead in trespasses and the uncircumcision of your flesh, God made alive together with him, having forgiven us our trespasses" (Colossians 2:12–13).

# Chapter Eight

### SHE MADE A VERY POISONOUS APPLE

*~ The Con in Contraception ~*

Who doesn't like to sprinkle life with some sweet goodness? One way I do this is by baking. Since I was small, I have been doing so. At some point, I promoted myself from box-kit baking to creating cake from scratch. This may have been a mistake. My premier pursuit was carrot cake. It was a rather easy recipe to follow: two cups of flour to make the sponge-like texture: two teaspoons of baking soda to make it rise; four eggs to make it moist; three cups of carrots to make it, well, carrot cake; and an array of other ingredients to promote deliciousness. This sugary delight soon became a specialty, but things did not start off so sweet. You see, the first time I fused fixings together, I managed to miss one major ingredient, one you really don't want to forget: sugar. The sculpted and sweet icing couldn't carry the baked-good–turned-bad. Thus, it looked enticing, but tasted horrible. After a sample, my dad was the first to discover this, and so the cake sat on the counter for days. No one had the heart to toss what I hoped would be my trophy cake. But some things should never be eaten, no matter how sweet they *appear*.

From the looks of things, Snow White also knows how to get busy with flour. In fact, unlike me, she appears to be quite the baking expert. (Piecrust from scratch has always impressed me.) When it comes to baking, however, some mixtures are more magical than others. For instance, while she was measuring and mixing a recipe, the wicked witch was doing some mixing of her own; "by the help of witchcraft,"[1] she was creating a polluted potion. The witch's brew is outside of any normal kitchen occurrence; it is spells and sorcery. Her recipe had toxic results. "Thereupon she went into a quite secret, lonely room, into which no one came, and there she made a very poisonous apple."[2] There is nothing sweet about the muddled mix. In fact, the concoction that the witch is conjuring is far from innocent. This isn't just baking, but brewing. Moreover, it is a dually destructive potion: to herself and her unsuspecting opponent. As for you, take note! Do not fall prey to any bewitching blend. You see, society is trying to sell you a spell, as well. It has a different notion about a potion that is in motion. And believe me, there is nothing sweet about it.

What potion am I referencing? Wrapped in a petite pill or patch, it is called contraception. Stick with me here. The wicked witch's potion was designed to produce death in the fair Snow White, so is this potion. Why? Well, the very name exposes just what it is, as Kimberly Hahn explains:

> *Contra* means "against"; *ceptus* refers to "conception," or the beginning of life. God made humankind, male and female, in his image. Satan cannot create as God does, so he seeks to mar or even destroy God's image. God is the life-giving Lover, the Spirit of Life. Satan is the life-hating destroyer, the spirit of antilife.[3]

We see this all throughout Scripture. God's love overflows into new life through creating, and Satan prowls about seeking to destroy life. From the very beginning of time, life has been seen as a very good thing and procreation a command from God. God Blessed Adam and Eve, saying, "Be fruitful and multiply; fill the earth and subdue it" (Genesis 1:28). After the flood when the ark was docked, God repeated his message of life: "God blessed Noah and his sons and said to them 'Be fruitful and multiply; fill the earth'" (Genesis 9:1). When using contraception, couples cannot fulfill this command. Contraception is, in reality, not so sweet.

Furthermore, one of God's promises to Abraham, the father of the Israelites, was a multitude of descendants: "Look toward heaven, and number the stars...so shall your descendants be" (Genesis 15:5). Abundant descendants are a gift. Unlike the modern world, Abraham did not fear that the environment would not sustain so many descendants; he knew God would take care of everything. He trusted. In the first chapter of Exodus, we see the firstfruits of God's covenant with Abraham: "The descendants of Israel [the chosen people] were fruitful and increased greatly" (Exodus 1:7). In contrast, we also see in the same chapter the corrupt ruler of the time attacking life and encouraging two midwives to kill all newborn boys. The Pharaoh did not get his way as "the midwives feared God, and did not do as the king of Egypt commanded them, but let the male children live" (Exodus 1:17). Those who love God must love life. Contraception is not so sweet.

Furthermore, women who were unable to have children never viewed it as a good thing; instead, barren women, such as Sarah (see Genesis 21:1–3), Hannah (see 1 Samuel 1:6–8), and Elizabeth (see Luke 1:7), all longed to have a child. God answered their diligent prayers and filled their wombs with new life. "He gives barren woman a home, /

making her the joyous mother of children. / Praise the Lord!" (Psalm 113:9). Thus, women should never seek to intentionally make themselves sterile, by which they surrender the precious gift of motherhood. Fertility is a sign of a healthy body, not an unhealthy one.

Contraception is not a modern issue, but a reoccurring one since the beginning of time (see Genesis 38:9). Even after Christ's coming, contraception remained a temptation. Back then, it was known specifically as a type of sorcery. A Scripture verse from the New Testament that is worth reviewing states, "Now the works of the flesh are plain: immorality, impurity, licentiousness, idolatry, *sorcery*...and the like. I warn you, as I warned you before, that those who do such things shall not inherit the kingdom of God" (Galatians 5:19–21, emphasis added). Stay with me for a minute, as you wonder what this verse has to do with contraception. The Greek (which is one of the first languages the Bible was written in) word for sorcery is *pharmakeia*. Certainly, that word reminds us of the word *pharmaceuticals* or drugs, and this is exactly what the Greek word signifies. In biblical times, "*pharmakeia* in general was the mix of various potions for secret purposes, including potions to prevent or stop pregnancy. The typical translation of the term *sorcery* is inadequate. When *pharmakeia* is condemned in Galatians 5:19–26 and Revelation 9:21 and 21:8, the context is sexual immorality or sexual immorality and murder. It is therefore reasonable to apply these passages to the condemnation of drugs used for contraception and abortion."[4] In Galatians 5:19, not only is sorcery condemned, it is regarded as a "work of the flesh." The first thing that comes to mind with the word *flesh* is our human body, of course. Thus, the sins listed have to do with acts of the body. Moreover, "works of the flesh" can be understood as acts that spring from our corrupt or fallen nature for sin that brought darkness into the world. Contraception is also a work of the flesh. Contraception is not so sweet.

Even after the close of the canon of Scripture (public revelation ended with the death of the last apostle, John), the early Church fathers (those who succeeded the apostles) spoke out against the use of birth control:

> The having of children they esteem grievous and unwelcome. Many at least with this view have paid money to be childless, and have mutilated nature, not only killing the newborn, but even acting to prevent their beginning to live (sterilization). Why do you sow where the field is eager to destroy the fruit, where there are medicines of sterility, where there is murder before birth?… Indeed, it is something worse than murder, and I do not know what to call it; for she does not kill what is formed but prevents its formation. Do you condemn the gift of God and fight with his (natural) laws? (John Chrysostom, A.D. 391)

> Who is he who cannot warn that no woman may take a *potion* so that she is unable to conceive or condemns in herself the nature which God willed to be fecund? As often as she could have conceived at birth, of that many homicides she will be held guilty, and unless she undergoes suitable penance, she will be damned by eternal death in hell. If a woman does not wish to have children, let her enter into a religious agreement with her husband; for chastity is the sole sterility of a Christian woman. (Caesarius, A.D. 522, emphasis added)

In fact, until 1931, *all* Christian denominations condemned the use of birth control. However, when an assembly of Anglican bishops gathered at what is known as the Lambeth Conference, all that changed. Together, the Anglican community deemed it permissible to use contraception if couples had serious reason to do so. Within a few years, all denominations approved the use of birth control and no longer asked for couples to establish the reason for it. Thus, the usage of contraception went from being rare to being the norm. Yet, the Catholic Church still stood firm in condemning contraception because the Church has always been an advocate of truth. Contraception is not so sweet.

In 1968, Holy Mother Church provided further guidance to its flock about birth control through a document known as *Humanae Vitae*, which is Latin for "Human Life." In this encyclical, Pope Paul VI explored God's plan for marital union and shared the detriments of contraception for families and society. Pope Paul VI predicted a great deal about what would happen if contraception were embraced, which included: an increase of marital infidelity, a lowering of moral standards, that man will forget the reverence due to a woman, woman will be reduced to an instrument for the satisfaction of men's desires, governments would use forced contraception to achieve their own agendas, abortion will become widespread, and since life is not reverenced, euthanasia will become a standard practice.[5] Indeed, all of these predictions have come to fruition. Amazing how destructive one little potion, that is, *pill* can be! Such sorcery will not lead to sainthood. Contraception is not so sweet.

In *Snow White*, the witch asks the princess, "Are you afraid of poison?"[6] Like the crafted apple, contraception is poison to the body. It carries a great deal of negative side effects and risks to those that use it, including blood clots, heart attack, breast cancer, stroke, cervical cancer, infertility, and weight gain. Sound good to you? Some pills not only prevent pregnancy but also cause an early abortion.[7] Today, certain pills contain a lower dose of hormones in hopes of decreasing side effects; however, this causes "more chances of breakthrough ovulation.

If this happens, it is possible for the egg to be fertilized, creating a new human life. The mother will be unaware that her new baby is unable to implant, and she will unknowingly have an abortion."[8] Contraception is not so sweet.

To understand further why contraception is wrong, let us turn to an analogy. If you were at a birthday party and you were served a big slice of, I don't know, carrot cake, but you were trying to avoid adding any extra cushioning to your hips, the normal choice to support your personal effort would be to refrain from eating a slice. However, if you took the slice, chucked the fork, and proceeded to lick your slice of cake, you would probably get a lot of shocked, grossed out looks. Why? Because that would be weird! Even if you gave the explanation that you wanted to enjoy the taste of the food without the consequence of calories, the crowd would not find this any more normal, and you'd probably never be invited to a party again. You see, the purpose of food is twofold: It is for both enjoyment and nourishment. God gave us taste buds as part of that enjoyment, and he gave us stomachs to break down the food and provide a way to give energy to the body.

That's why certain eating issues are referred to as disorders. Take bulimia, for example. Someone with this problem indulges in a ton of food, but later vomits it up. The world understands that this is a severe problem, something that distorts God's design for food.

The same is true when it comes to sexual intimacy. Designed to be reserved for marriage, its purpose is also twofold: for both unity and procreation. Therefore, separating the procreative element from the enjoyment of sexual intimacy is also disordered. In fact, "these two meanings or values of marriage cannot be separated without altering the couple's spiritual life and compromising the goods of marriage and the future of the family" (*CCC* 2363). Just like with food, "if we feast on the love of each other and seek to vomit the contents of our love (or fertility), we are thwarting the natural law, and our act is disordered."[9] God is not random. He made everything with a purpose in mind, be it our stomach or our sexuality. Instead of embracing God's design for sexuality in its entirety, the procreative aspect is being controlled. The gift of sex in marriage is about entering into a deeper union with your spouse, while being open to the fruits of that love. It is an acceptance and openness to the entire person, including each spouse's fertility. It is about love and responsibility. Moreover, it is about God's plan, not our plans. Contraception is not so sweet.

In using contraception, a couple falls prey to all the same tactics that Snow White did when she was tempted, which we've seen include desire, intimidation, and doubt. The desires for contraception can be far-ranging: a desire to be in control, a desire to map out the course of life, a desire to place a career over the divine call to be a mother, a desire for pleasure without responsibility, a desire for acquiring stuff instead of helping create souls, a desire to be self-serving instead of self-giving. Intimidation and doubt take shape when a couple sees pregnancy as a risk, not a gift, and they allow doubt to creep in. Instead of trusting God, they look to the world. What will others say if we have so many children? How could we afford to feed all those mouths? Can the world sustain such large families? The answer to all these questions is never birth control. Contraception is not so sweet.

However, that is not to say that the Church does not encourage responsible parenting. The Church teaches something called Natural Family Planning (NFP), which is a way to remain open to life, while being responsible stewards of life through periods of abstinence within marriage. This method looks at a woman's fertility, as she is able to have children only during certain times of the month. What makes this different from contraception? Nothing unnatural is used to prevent a birth, and prayerful discernment between the spouses about their personal circumstances is ongoing. Furthermore, as stated in the encyclical *Humanae Vitae*, "If therefore there are well-grounded reasons for spacing births, arising from the physical or psychological condition of husband or wife, or from external circumstances, the Church teaches that married people may then take advantage of the natural cycles immanent in the reproductive system and engage in marital intercourse only during those times that are infertile, thus controlling birth in a way which does not in the least offend the moral principles."[10] I have provided a very brief description of NFP. In preparation for marriage, it would be worthwhile to read up more on what the Church teaches about NFP: what it is, what it is not, how to use it, when it is permissible to use it, and how to use it. The Church has a lot of holy wisdom to share.

Let us look at the recipe of our lives. May it be mixed with wholesome ingredients and filled with sweet choices. Indeed, "The law of the Lord is perfect, / reviving the soul… / the ordinances of the Lord are true, / and righteous altogether. / More to be desired are they than gold, / even much fine gold; / *sweeter* also than honey / and drippings of the honeycomb" (Psalm 19:7, 10–11, emphasis added). True sweetness is found in Christ, in his law, his ways, and his plan for our lives, not by using contraception. Trust in him!

# Part Two

• ~ • ~ •

## CINDERELLA

"The young girl swept, baked, and washed for the whole household.
She wore only shabby clothes."[1]
—*The Brothers Grimm*

• ~ • ~ •

## Chapter Nine

### HOW CAN I GO TO THE BALL LIKE THIS?
#### ~ Fitting Fashion ~

Once, I snuck into my mother's closet one week before my birthday. This was, of course, a horrible idea. These four walls housed my gifts, and I made sure to scour the shelves and make note of everything I was getting. I saw what was not yet mine to see. It felt wrong. In hopes of avoiding suspicion, I began practicing my surprised face. Before my acting debut, my parents found out about what I had done. Guilt set in. They told me they had returned all the gifts. Disappointment reigned. That year I learned, but I think I knew all along, that mysteries are worth keeping veiled until they can be revealed properly.

Why is it that we gift wrap boxes? It is because there is great intrigue and excitement when you're giving or are greeted by a beautifully wrapped box dressed in shimmery paper and a bright bow. Gift boxes that look crumpled or half-wrapped show little care for the hidden object inside. Forget about pretty wrapping. Why bother wrapping at all?

We wrap to give our gifts character, to express a certain personality, and to keep the object inside a secret and the anticipation high.

We bedazzle our boxes for the sake of a pretty presentation. Some may even say the wrapping is a gift in itself. If we had the option between receiving a gift that was wrapped, half wrapped, or altogether unwrapped...surely, we would choose the wrapped one. But if we take pride in a simple material object, why is it that many of us aren't doing such a good job with our own wrapping, or what we more commonly term clothing? Ours looks tampered with and sparse. Mystery has fled. Do you appear as a half-wrapped gift?

Despite what the culture says and demonstrates, the reality is that women are called to veil their bodies. Why? Because their beauty is such a special gift! For example, a bride wears a veil on her wedding day, not because she is ugly, but because she is radiant. On my wedding day, I wore a traditional veil called a blusher; the sheer fabric hung like a delicate haze in front of my face. For added mystery, I also wore a second veil that draped down to my waist and was made of diaphanous tulle and a fringe of fine lace and tasteful sparkles. The act of veiling is a symbolic way of tantalizing the groom because the bride conceals her beauty until they are officially wed and he is permitted to see her. To further demonstrate this idea, let's look to sacred Scripture.

In the book of Genesis, we have the love story between Isaac and Rebekah. Through divine providence, Rebekah became Isaac's wife. Abraham, the father of Isaac, sent out a servant in search of a wife for his son and, through prayer, the servant was able to discern whom God willed for Isaac. Eventually, Rebekah is asked if she will marry Isaac and, foreshadowing Our Lady's *fiat*,[1] Rebecca accepts the will of God as her own. Isaac and Rebekah had never met, but she trusted in God's plan for her life. We too can relate to this story, trusting that God has a special person in mind for us. However, this soul mate situation is not what struck me most about this Old Testament account.

What I like most about this story is Rebekah's first reaction to her soon-to-be husband. After journeying from afar, Rebekah finally comes across her beloved to be. "And Rebekah lifted up her eyes and when she saw Isaac, she alighted from her camel and said to the servant, 'Who is the man yonder, walking through the fields to meet us?' The servant said, 'That is my master.' So she took her veil and covered herself. The servant recounted to Isaac all the things he had done. Then Isaac brought her into the tent; and took Rebekah, and she became his wife" (Genesis 24:64–67). Did you catch that? Rebekah is just *mere* moments away from marrying Isaac, and yet she *still* seeks to veil herself. She understands the importance of the mystery and gift that she is as a woman.

Rebekah demonstrates that "modesty protects the intimate center of a person. It means refusing to unveil what should remain hidden" (*CCC* 2521). We should heed this lovely example of modesty! Our bodies, like Rebekah's, are sacred. "Do you not know that your body is a temple of the Holy Spirit within you, which you have from God? You are not your own; you were bought with a price. So glorify God in your body" (1 Corinthians 6:19–20). One important way this is done is through the veil of clothes. In this way, veils are not just for brides on their wedding days, but for our every day. After all, as members of the Church, we are all brides of our Bridegroom, Christ. Sacred Scripture gives this advice to men: "Turn away your eyes from a shapely woman, / and do not look intently at beauty belonging to another" (Sirach 9:8). Indeed, certain intimate elements of a woman's beauty belong only to the man who will be her husband. We are a gift to remain wrapped until we are wed. Culture, of course, has torn down tradition and truth, and has left us baring it all.

In *Cinderella*, the first scene of the movie is quite cute, and worth watching closely. Two little blue birdies sing softly to wake the blonde beauty. Once up, the princess sings a tune about her dreams, and this beckons her other animal friends to join her. All are drawn to her graceful beauty. As Cinderella continues in song, she begins to get ready for the day. If we watch closely, we see some important reactions to this morning routine. Some animals sway in song, while others are told they cannot stay. Who is shooed out of the scene? The *male* mice.[2] Until the last bow is tied, Cinderella's body is blanketed from the wrong kind of spectators, the opposite sex; ours should be, too.

Was this merely a more innocent time, or are Cinderella and her female friends onto something? Let us focus on what Cinderella seems to be aware of. In chapter six, some of the differences of males and females were discussed. However, I want to dedicate a little more time to discussing one main difference. It is important for ladies to understand that guys are visual; not visual in the "I like to match colors" way, but visual in the "I notice women's bodies" way. Basically, "even decent guys who are happily 'going with' a girl are instinctively pulled to want to visually take in, linger on, and fantasize about all the details of an attractive girl's body."[3] Therefore, guys will stare at girls even if it is out of the corner of their eye—and they usually aren't focused on their faces. Furthermore, if a girl is dressed in a way "to call attention to her figure, he's strongly tempted to picture her naked."[4] Yikes! Of course things get more difficult the more skin a woman exposes and the tighter her clothing. This news is a bit shocking, but good to know when it comes to how we ladies deck out our bodies, and the impact that has.

Here is an odd example to help you relate: If a clerk had a big ugly pimple on his face, you probably couldn't help but stare directly at it.

You might not want to, but your eyeballs would be drawn to it. He has eyes, eyebrows, a nose, and a mouth, and all you can stare at is that big red dot on his face! Now, women's body parts are far from pimples, but if they are exposed, the same visual struggle takes place for a guy. Don't believe me? Study a man's face the next time an immodestly dressed woman walks in his vicinity. Your clothes have consequences. "Many have been misled by a woman's beauty, / and by it passion is kindled like a fire" (Sirach 9:8). For men, immodest outfits are not only a lure of lust but more importantly a temptation to treat you like an object instead of the person, body and soul, that you are. This is an ugly truth that many ladies don't want to digest, and we have a hard time understanding since we don't possess the same struggle.

On the flip side, women are more emotional than visual. We like a handsome face, nice hair, and a guy who dresses well, even good cologne, but ladies don't usually daydream about a guy's figure. In fact, we'd rather not. Instead, we like to collect daydreams of the way he might treat us and what he might say. It is important for men to take this into account. However, it would be wrong for any man to use this knowledge in a manipulative way. For instance, if you had a big crush on someone, call him Johnny, and one day Johnny came up to you and poured out compliments upon you, and told you he was falling for you…what would you do? You would probably be beside yourself and really excited. But what if, just as you were beginning to melt in this bliss, Johnny turned to you and said it was all a joke. You'd be humiliated, upset, and feel teased. Moreover, you certainly wouldn't want Johnny to brush off how he hurt you by declaring that girls need to toughen up their emotions. If you wouldn't want a guy to toy with your emotions, don't toy with his visual vulnerability!

So don't write this off as a "guy problem" alone, while blowing off your accountability. Keep in mind that "if a girl's clothes choice doesn't show off her body, the guy's temptation usually doesn't get triggered."[5] You can call guys perverts, or you can be sensitive to their struggle and seek to preserve your dignity by what you wear. Build up your brothers in Christ by shrouding yourself in the right kind of threads.

Aside from not previously knowing, or perhaps not accepting, how men and women are wired differently, what else motivates a gal's ensemble? The possibilities are many, but one struggle among women is insecurity and a poor body image. In the area of apparel, this has an impact in two ways. For some girls, they simply do not believe that any man would desire to look at them. Ladies may think: *I've got chicken legs, I have a flat chest, I have a chubby tummy, I am big-boned, I have acne, my nose is too big, I am short, I am too tall, I have a weird body shape,* and on and on and on. Maybe you have had one or more similar thoughts yourself. Thus, someone with such a view of themselves might think that wearing a short skirt is no problem at all. Despite any woman or young girl's body image, or your own image of yourself, trust me—as a young woman, no matter the size, shape, or maturity, you *are* beautiful, and you *are* noticed simply because you are a female (the apex of creation!). Debate all you want, but women are gorgeous and men's eyes are on us. The scary truth is that this isn't just guys your age, but men of *all* ages. That might be creepy to think about, too, but it should make you all the more aware. No lady wants someone's grandpa winking at her for the wrong reasons! Therefore, this insecure and naïve mind-set simply cannot guide your garb.

For other women, their negative self-image encourages them to stoop to immodesty for a different reason. For example, such a lady may not think she has the prettiest face, but knows that if she wears a low-cut shirt or tight jeans, she will win attention. Her overall insecurity encourages her to isolate certain body parts to gain a guy's glance. Yes, every woman wants to be noticed. However, deep down, no one wants to beg for attention. Each woman simply wants to be beautiful and be regarded for who she is and not for what she shows or how she suits. Dress yourself in clothes that retain and crown your mystery, and encourage others to do likewise! Be noticed for the right reasons.

Other girls have a wonderful body image, and a sister, their mother, a close friend, or perhaps their own popular status may have even encouraged this view. Great! Insecurities shouldn't weigh us down, and we should be confident in how God has made us. Nevertheless, the motto "protect your prettiness" should still be stamped upon the soul. I have heard some moms say to their daughters, "If you've got it, flaunt it! You're only young once." This is completely the wrong idea. Can you imagine if someone did this with their riches by using wads of cash as fans, and wearing enough bling to weigh anyone down? We'd find that obnoxious! Women should never manipulate the men in their lives by way of their garments or lack thereof. In other words, don't use your breasts, butt, or any other body part as a compass of control when you stroll in the presence of the opposite sex. Your valuable body deserves to be veiled, respected, and presented in a worthy manner.

Speaking of clothes…let's talk shopping. As a kid, I hated clothes. What was I thinking? On birthdays, if I thought I was getting an article of clothing, I'd push the box aside and open it last. However, as I grew up, shopping became a hobby. Clothes became prized objects! My closet couldn't wait to receive them—with its big square arms seemingly outstretched to receive the blouses, dresses, jeans, and sweaters I would bring. Beginning in the teen years, most ladies love to shop. There are many places to go, but malls are the top option. Malls are like amusement parks for girls—miles of name brands, glowing shop windows with spotlighted goodies, colorful advertisements, mannequins dressed in the latest and the greatest, blaring upbeat music, smiles, deals, heels, and meals found in the food court. Malls are magnetic, and everything and everyone seems to whisper "Spend, spend, spend!" And the clothes practically reach out to you, longing for you to take them home.

The mall experience can certainly be entrancing and enticing. With that said, it is no wonder that what is presented in shop windows shapes, or perhaps blurs, our view of fashion. It should be noted how little most of the clothes displayed for purchase actually cover up. And while the plastic people that wear these garments have no shame, real people should. Overall, malls don't empower modesty or Christians. Instead, such a place discourages it and us. Finding a non-revealing fashionable frock in the stores can feel harder than finding a needle in a haystack. If you have tried, you know it is an exhausting experience, and if you haven't, you have work to do! That's not to say the hunt is hopeless. With perseverance, tasteful treasures can be found. But, on the whole, malls are just another lure to immodesty for ladies, and the commodity of clothes, hung from hangers, might as well be little red dangling apples. We are allured, and we are eating, that is, *wearing*, what we shouldn't. It is time to cut down the apple tree and flee from what you thought was a shopping paradise.

If we walk through a mall and allow secular fashion to feed us, we end up dismissing modesty. Yet, modesty is the solution. It "inspires a way of life which makes it possible to resist the allurements of fashion and pressures of prevailing ideologies" (*CCC* 2523). Overall, the fashion industry tells us that if we don't wear what they are selling, we will be unfashionable. Lie! Most girls don't want to stray too far from what's deemed popular or name brand because they fear they will not fit in. Or perhaps, you have given in because you realize it takes more work to search through the racks of clothes to find something that covers what it should. Don't let fleeting fashions strip you of your hems or get your dignity down. Have confidence in being a Christian. A change of culture begins with you. In retaining mystery, you won't sacrifice looking good. Modesty isn't for hiding, and it is not reserved for old people who are past their prime. It is for each one of God's precious daughters. It is for you. Are you ready to toss out what really isn't fitting for someone of faith?

Saying good-bye to favorites isn't easy, but the purging process is important to do. You will be ready to do this when you truly lift up your heart to Christ. You see, modesty begins with an overall conversion. Otherwise, you will just see it as another set of rules and restrictions. Modesty is tied to the heart; it is just one more way to love Christ. "Purity of heart will enable us to see God: It enables us even now to see things according to God" (*CCC* 2531). You cannot truly be connected to Christ and dress in a way that is more pagan than pure. When you are tied to your Father in Heaven, you will grow and change. Aspects of your life will be brought into the light, your eyes will be opened to a deeper conversion, and your heart will long to conform more truly to Christ. Beginning now, may Christ be your sun, which illuminates your way, ways, and wardrobe.

Overall, fashion is a conversation. What are you saying to the world about who you are, and what you are about? Express yourself well and consistently, be it your everyday outfit, a sports jersey, swimsuit, Sunday best, or a dress for an elegant evening out. It is important to be stead-fast in the modesty mission. Modesty is an invitation to bear authentic witness to Jesus as a woman by displaying your dignity in the way you dress. Whereas, "the fashions of the day are geared toward destroying women's sensitivity for the dignity of their sex."[6] As Catholics, we are familiar with the sacraments. One definition of a sacrament is that it is a sign of Christ (see *CCC* 774). Your clothes, like a sacrament, are also a sign. Therefore, don't be a walking contradiction, but rather, be a sign of value and virtue. Avoid distracting people from viewing your heart and seeing the sparkle of your soul by isolating one or two body parts. Instead, frame your heart and your face in order to reflect your truest beauty.

Let's look to Cinderella to see how she does this. It all begins with an exciting announcement that "the king's son made up his mind to give a ball, and to invite to it all people of fashion."[7] Cinderella begins plotting what she might wear. Up the stairs she climbs to her room in the tower, and from a trunk she pulls out a dress that once belonged to her mother. She admits that maybe it is a little old-fashioned. (But hey, in my opinion, there is nothing wrong with retro if you know how to tweak it into trendy.) Cinderella searches a book for a classy make-over, declaring her plan to update it, which includes a sash, a ruffle, and collar accessories. She certainly seems knows how to spruce up her find with the right accoutrements.

In enacting modesty, creativity is key. Like Cinderella, it is good to know how to update a garment or how to accessorize and layer an outfit. (Tips to come!) Also, in order to gain the right kind of ideas, Cinderella knows her go-to resource. We too should have a mental file of what places will appropriately inspire our embellishments. Gaining ideas and inspiration doesn't have to cost you a dollar. Also, if you are feeling extra resourceful and are up for a scavenger hunt, I encourage thrift store shopping because vintage is fashionable these days. Of course you can also stick to department stores, but if you brave the mall, be discerning of what shops should be on your list of stops.

On your outings, search for outfits that cover what they should and avoid clothes that hug what they shouldn't. Basically, this means it shouldn't be too short (one inch above the knee is my cut off, which goes for shorts and skirts.), or too low (four fingers below the collar bone is my base line), and isn't too tight or see-through. Also, I suggest avoiding tank tops and shirts that do not cover your shoulders. These simple tips will definitely help you live out modesty. I find that simple, solid-color shirts are the best when it comes to building a base for modest outfits (but not the only way). From there, you can find great necklaces, hair accessories, bows, boots, leggings, sweaters, scarves, and shoes to deck out an outfit. Layering makes for a fun and fresh expression and is helpful in boosting your outfit's color bouquet, while helping with modesty. These tips allow you to be uniquely your own and remain fashionable, while not offending your heavenly Prince Charming, Jesus Christ.

Now, let's turn to Cinderella's flock of friends for some more motivation in the fashion field. When Cinderella gets bogged down with chores by her stepfamily, her mice friends decide to take on her fashion project, which is the dress for the ball. In particular, two of her friends really help out, as Jaq and Gus go out looking for the trimmings for the dress. During their shopping spree, they have some interesting encounters. Both stepsisters are throwing articles of clothing to the ground and stomping in sass, while declaring their dresses to be "old rags," and their accessories "trash." These sisters demonstrate a pagan culture that is restless, greedy, has a disposable mentality, and is often uncreative. After the tantrum, a pile of waste remains, and the mice attempt to collect this seemingly unwanted apparel for Cinderella. This is not an easy task with the household cat nearby, who just so happens to have the name Lucifer.

Just like these little mice with a mission, your hunt won't always be easy. For them, and you, there is a very big cat in the midst of things: "Your adversary the devil prowls around like a roaring lion, seeking some one to devour" (1 Peter 5:8). Just like Lucifer the cat who gets caught in the clothes, the devil also uses clothing in his hungry hunt. Modesty won't be easy when the devil knows that immodesty is ammunition to destroy souls. His threats may come in many forms, such as insecurities, peer pressure, doubt, laziness, and a variety of desires. Don't let him prey upon you. Instead, may you pray to Christ and ask him to help you be an aid, not a hindrance, in building up others and yourself in holiness. "The power that women can wield over men is great indeed. If they pursue their own selfish aims, women are Satan's slaves. If they put their charm at God's service, they are *God's great allies*."[8]

Let's turn to *Cinderella* again. At the end of the day, the stepmother feels victorious in her scheming to prevent Cinderella from attending the ball. However, a surprise comes when Cinderella returns to her quarters to find the fruits of her friends' labors. Next we see her in pink prancing down the staircase to catch up to her stepfamily. They are clearly not excited at the sight of her or at the idea of her accompanying them.

Feeling threatened by the trendsetter, the head of this pack of wolves, the stepmother, attacks. Walking up to Cinderella, she points out the accessories, which the mice collected, to her daughters. After the stepmother's sly prompting, the stepsisters realize Cinderella's outfit features their recycled goods. They angrily respond verbally, but the attack soon becomes physical as they shout and begin to pull upon the beads and bows. They unwrap her, tearing layer after layer, until

Cinderella is left in fabric scraps, with her dress destroyed.[9] After they are done, she appears as a half-wrapped gift, which she never intended to be.

In reality, society's standards will leave you in tatters, too. Cinderella's response is tears. She is too embarrassed to go to the ball. More ladies should share her sentiments. Yet, "the fashion world (has) systematically attempt(ed) to eradicate in girls the 'holy bashfulness' which is the proper response that women should give to what is personal, intimate, and calls for veiling."[10]

Dismayed, Cinderella runs to the garden. Certainly, she is not the first to be attacked for her beauty or modesty. Like some, she feels discouraged, and her faith weakened. In tears, she speaks aloud saying, "I wish I could. I wish I could."[11] In a warm glow, her fairy godmother appears and responds, "You wish that you could go to the ball; is it not so?"[12] Once the godmother's wand is found, the fashion festivities begin. A pumpkin turns into a fine white coach, and mice to horses. She is also provided with a coachman and footman.

At first, the godmother overlooks Cinderella's damaged dress. Therefore, Cinderella questions her about her dress, "How can I go to the ball like this?"[13] In her fog, the godmother almost lets Cinderella go out in unfitting fashion. However, we all need to shake off our fashion fog, realizing immodesty isn't lovely. Quickly, she regains her senses, and declares that Cinderella "shall soon be more beautiful than her coach."[14]

Yes, we all need a good mentor to offer us advice about what is truly best for us—or mentally smack some sense into us. We might not have fairy godmothers, but we do have the Holy Mother Church. She has plenty of wisdom in her wings. Look to her, and those who declare her teachings. Hang on to what you learn in order to have high standards.

Clearly the godmother has high standards for her daughter. "Tapping Cinderella lightly with her wand…Cinderella's old clothes were turned into robes of silk and velvet, glittering with jewels. And the fairy godmother gave her a little pair of shining glass slippers, the prettiest that ever were seen."[15]

Here is a wise woman. She knows how to dress Cinderella in something that fits her body type and her coloring, and she is willing to push the fashion bar with a bit of a dare. Cinderella emerges stunning and modest, and all in attendance at the ball are struck by her beauty.[16] We too can accomplish beauty and modesty at once. It is all in the wrapping.

# Chapter Ten

## WE LIKE YOU
### ~ *Friendship* ~

The night of my rehearsal dinner had arrived, which meant my walk to the altar was shortening. Just a few yards away from it now. My dad would deliver me, and my bridesmaids would be there at my side, seven in total. These were the women I called dear friends: each one so different from the next, each one bringing out a different aspect of my personality, and each one a unique blessing. We had laughed together, cried together, prayed together, and journeyed together. Supporting one another through life's moments came naturally, and so did simply enjoying one another's company, wherever life took us, be it trips, muddy ATV rides, "snow-pocalypses," chats over warm tea, nights out or in, holidays, and birthdays.

I had prayed hard to find such beloved Christ-centered friends, and here they were all in one room. What an occasion! Butterflies of the next day aside, this was a moment I wanted to reflect on just how much each one of my friends meant to me. So I stood before them, with my hand clasped by another friend, my soon-to-be husband, and shared how thankful I was for each one of them. Along with Christ, family, and all of life's experiences, they had helped nurture me into the woman my dad would give away the next day.

Perhaps this moment, which caused me to reflect, was held so special in my heart because it wasn't always this way. In fact, it had taken a long time to find such amazing friends, years really. The truth is, *authentic* friendships are rare. Scripture describes such friendships as "treasures" (Sirach 6:14). But why? Is God holding back on us? No, God wants to bless you, I promise. Shouldn't such a good and beautiful thing be found in abundance? Yes, but we can thank original sin and concupiscence for our struggle on a variety of fronts, including this one. If you don't have a lot of friends, is there something wrong with you? No, there just might be something very *right* with you. Is there a secret to friendship? I think so. If you stick with me, we will uncover it.

At this point in your life, you may feel several different things. You may feel you have a great many friends. Or perhaps, you feel you only have several friends. Or maybe, you think you don't have many friends at all, and feel a bit lonely. Maybe there are plenty of people around you, but you sense you cannot genuinely share yourself with them. What is the reason for all of these possible scenarios?

Let's snatch a scene from *Cinderella*, when a group of mice assemble to share that a new mouse has been spotted in a trap. Upon being rescued by Cinderella, the mouse goes from shaking solo straight into solidarity. The fellow mice boost the nervous newbie's confidence with assurance of their sentiments, saying simply that he is liked. The friendship is inaugurated. Like most friendships, this one begins with a mutual liking of one another, but there is much more to making friends than just that.

How do we build friendships? Most often, there is a shared interest that unites us. This could mean being a part of the same youth group, marching band, soccer team, dance class, photography club, or any other favorite activity. Though you may enjoy all the participants in such groups, you may become close with a select few after determining that you have additional uniting interests. Most likely, you will bond even more with someone after a mutual experience—like sharing several classes together, a retreat weekend, an extended class trip, a weeklong summer camp, or being college roommates. Spending extended time with someone through similar experiences strengthens the connection. Such moments also help people feel more comfortable and willing to share, providing the necessary time and grounds to cultivate good conversation.

But there still seems to be something more to building worthwhile friendships. Having the kind of friends that can own the title "treasure" takes something very specific. Are you ready for the secret? It is virtue. Yes, virtue. It makes so much sense, really, but in order to understand why, you might need a refresher course in what exactly a virtue is.

Good habits become virtues. For instance, fasting from potato chips and ice cream scoops during Lent if done habitually through the forty days may result in building up the virtue of temperance. Overall, a virtue is described as "a habitual and firm disposition to do the good" (*CCC* 1803). Simply knowing what is right and wrong is not enough to make a person virtuous. Instead, "virtues are all about *living out* the truth that you know."[1] Virtues require action, not just knowledge. This turning toward the good should be reflected in our thoughts, actions, and reactions. "Genuine friendship—by definition—requires such traits as honesty, trust, loyalty, goodwill, and sacrifice. These are qualities that are consistently found in men and women of good character."[2] A person doesn't simply wake up with virtues; developing them takes work! Furthermore, the "goal of a virtuous life is to become like God" (*CCC* 1803). Thus, Christ is truly reflected in the virtuous person because they have come to know him through a personal relationship (see John 15:14).

Not only is virtue the root of any friendship worth keeping, Scripture also tells us that it is the key: "There is nothing so precious as a faithful friend, / and no scales can measure his excellence. / A faithful friend is an elixir of life; / and those who fear the Lord will find him. / Whoever fears the Lord directs his friendship aright, / for as he is, so is his neighbor" (Sirach 6:15–17). Is it making sense now? If we love and serve our Lord Jesus, and truly have a friendship with him in prayer, we will become like him. Moreover, those who have the same mission will be drawn to you. Christ is not just one more uniting interest. An interest in Jesus just so happens to serve as *the* foundation for great friendships. Virtue attracts others that share the same desire to be holy because "true friendship and virtue are inseparable; you cannot have one without the other."[3]

To understand the need for virtue in friendship, let's return to the scene of rescue in *Cinderella*, when Jaq introduces the new mouse to his fellow friends. Specifically, what does he share about Cinderella? The mouse shares that she is nice. Cinderella gives the chubby mouse a shirt, shoes, and a cute hat. Clearly, Cinderella welcomes him warmly and even gives him a name, Octavius, or Gus for short. All of this seems to be a manifestation of Cinderella's virtue, which means she has the makings of a true friend.

No offense to the sweet songbirds, mice, chickens, horse, and dog that serve as Cinderella's pals, but if Cinderella is so virtuous, why does it appear that she has trouble making friends with *people*? "Had she no friends in the world?"[4] Well, first, she obviously does not get out much. Second, the phrase "Birds of a feather flock together" is a perfectly fitting phrase in Cinderella's case. Her stepfamily might be considered kin, but they aren't of the same "feather." Cinderella seems to have more in common with birds than her own "fowl" family. And the main reason for the friendship barrier is that Cinderella lives by virtue, while her stepfamily operates by way of vice. They isolate and eventually lock Cinderella in a tower for a selfish agenda. They assign her endless chores and place constant demands upon her. They give her rags to wear, and, when threatened and jealous, they destroy her clothes and call her names.

Know anyone similar? Well, probably not by the exact profile, but "you will know them by their fruits" (Matthew 7:20). In other words, people's actions, be they good or bad, often reflect what is within their hearts—and reveal if they are capable of genuine friendship. Furthermore, "friends not only share each other's joys and sorrows, they are committed to each other and desire each other's good, their well being."[5] These qualities were not something that Cinderella's family ever exemplified, though her creature cohorts often did. The animal friends helped make her a dress, accompanied her to the ball in fresh form (thanks to the fairy godmother), and even risked their lives to unlock her from a tower. They lived the sentiment: "When you flourish, when you are blessed, I rejoice with you, for it is as though it is my flourishing and blessedness. When you fail or suffer, I fail and suffer."[6] Truly, these are noble friends.

Therefore, if virtue is the formula for friendship, and you seek it, you will probably have a difficult time connecting with those who are not in the market for it. If you are feeling cast aside, could it be that those around you are more connected by *vice* than by virtue? Just like Cinderella's stepfamily, these cliques, whether they realize it or not, are united by their vice—maybe self-absorption, a tendency toward rudeness, gossip, bad language, making fun of others, jealousy, promiscuity,

intemperance, or often simply a lack of Jesus in their lives. Often people
of vice will despise those seeking to live by virtue. Be strong, and never
sell out!

Unlike those who live by vice, a person of virtue is one who centers
"his or her life on what is truly good, as opposed to self-gratification,
is capable of an unselfish, other-centered stance."[7] Perhaps this is why
Cinderella, a woman of virtue, acted as a true servant toward others,
even those who did not treat her with charity. She was consistent in
virtue no matter the case, and this allowed her to be a real friend. What
kind of friend are you? And what kind of friends do you have?

What about friendships that begin in virtue, but change over time?
You may have been great friends with someone for a while but if their
values shift toward bad habits and they cast aside their morals, while
you stay true, you might have a hard time staying friends. In cases
like this, it can be difficult to let go, but unless you change for the
worse, which isn't recommended, it is worth admitting you just don't
gel anymore. With discernment, you will have to decide what Jesus
is asking of you. Do you need to reduce the time you spend with this
person? Cut off the friendship tactfully? Have a heart-to-heart talk?
Pray for them? Overall, it is good to know when to let go, and sometimes that is a painful experience. But if a relationship doesn't build
you up in what is truly good and beautiful, it is not worth forcing or
compromising your values.

To further understand this concept of what bonds, let's turn to the
Gospel. Now, Jesus didn't always hang out with those who were considered the town's saints: "And as he sat at table in the house, behold,
many tax collectors and sinners came and sat down with Jesus and
his disciples" (Matthew 9:10). Yes, Jesus dined with sinners, but for a
very specific reason: He was calling them out of their life of sin. Jesus

wanted to heal them (see Luke 5:31–32). Basically, Jesus is setting the example for our need to evangelize, encourage others to leave behind their old ways, and embrace a life of virtue instead of vice.

It's important to note that this is different than hanging out and becoming a close associate with people who seek to live outside of God's grace, and do not respond to Christ's invitation. Such a situation could prove destructive because the group may end up leading you astray, instead of you leading them toward Christ. There is no doubt that "it is with your friends that you form habits and develop your character."[8] Just like the stepsisters, "a bad friend is one with whom you share your life, but who draws you away from the truly good life, from virtue."[9] Pick your friends wisely!

To demonstrate this point further, try this: Stand on a chair, and then get someone to stand on the floor on one side of the chair. Next, attempt to pick up your volunteer by grabbing her arm with yours. You will find it difficult to raise someone up to your level. But now, ask her to try to pull you down from the chair. She will find it quite easy. To draw someone down is much easier—both physically and spiritually. Perhaps this is why the New Testament says, "Do not be deceived: 'Bad company ruins good morals'" (1 Corinthians 15:33).

Of course, just because two individuals are both virtuous does not necessarily mean that they will automatically be friends, for often "it is not a person's virtue that we notice right away. The first thing we notice is that we happen to like them."[10] One's personality and temperament "play just as large as a role in friendship as does one's virtue."[11]

In addition to "virtuous friendships," two other kinds of friendship are "pleasant friendship" and "useful friendship." The focus in a pleasant friendship is simply that you enjoy your time together. Often, these types of relationships are formed with people you see on a regular basis because you are in a club together or on the same team, and you enjoy each other's company. "This friendship is basically about having a good time together. What each sees and values in the other is that the others is a cause of some pleasure for [her]self."[12]

A "useful friendship" is based on receiving some kind of profit from the other person. An example of this type would be if you tutored someone in math, and in exchange they gave you free dance lessons. Often, business relationships fall under this category of friendship. In both of these types of relationships, the basis of the association is not so much love for the person. Sometimes after discernment or certain interactions with a person, what we thought was a virtuous friendship might end up fitting into one of these two other categories instead. Or perhaps, a friendship that you saw simply as "pleasant" or "useful" may eventually become a deeper relationship.

Of course, even if you do not consider someone a close friend, you should still be friendly. As a Christian, it is important to be charitable and warm to others. When you run into someone you know, make sure you acknowledge them, say hello, smile, or simply wave, for hospitality is a virtue. Plus, you never know what may come out of the budding relationship. Old friends are particularly special because you have built a history together (see Sirach 9:10), but also be open to forming new bonds. You never know whom God wants to bring into your life.

Lastly, remember that you can be the spark that starts a friendship. Do not feel like you have to wait for others to talk to you, or invite you to something. If you are hoping to form deeper bonds with an individual or group, why not host an event? Suck up any insecurity you have, and do it! This could be pizza and a movie at your house, or perhaps something seasonal like a pumpkin-carving party or a canoe trip. A one-on-one "date," like coffee or a weekend lunch, is a great option, too. People love to be remembered and included, and you can be the one to make that happen.

In the end, the amount of effort and time that you put into your friendships will help determine the strength of your friendships. Build your close friendships on virtue and love, and, before you know it, years will have passed, and your freshly found friends will be your old beloved friends, just as mine were at my side on my wedding day.

# Chapter Eleven

## YOU MUST LEAVE THE BALL BEFORE
## THE CLOCK STRIKES TWELVE

### ~ Love and Honor ~

Every morning before the school bell rang, I'd walk through the red doors of my high school to find the halls packed with students. Yet, while my fellow peers gathered like glue at lockers, it was my opportunity to gawk; I had become a skilled observer of my crush. My actual school assignment was to study facts in books and on blackboards, but instead I studied every last feature upon the face I admired. I daydreamed of meeting him and of going to prom together. Was it love? No, of course not, just a girlish fantasy. But the feelings I had sure felt intense, though he and I had never actually spoken. Clearly my approach was unhealthy and ridiculous, but have you ever shared a similar scenario?

Looking back, my sentiments toward this handsome stranger were shallow. When excitement and emotion eclipse the heart, many of us mistake feelings of infatuation for love (sadly, sometimes over and over). Now that I grasp this, I want to help you avoid false forms of love. Often, we don't quite have an understanding of *true* love. This, of course, is not aided by the many poor examples illustrated in movies, TV shows, books, celebrity relationships, our peers, and perhaps our own families. Even our dear Cinderella can lead us to have confused ideas about what makes for a "happily ever after." All of these misguided examples have set us up to hope for and look for something that's not love.

Unquestionably, one of the dialogues of a woman's soul is romance. We long for a love to call our own. Romance is a good thing, but relationships should not be rushed into just to experience it. Unfortunately, patience is not always a language that gals are inclined to, but for true love it is a must. When the idyllic fever for a fellow strikes, it can lead to a foggy brain, and discernment gets dumped. It is as if we are in a dream state; Cinderella was. Her dreamy evening began with her own radiant transformation, followed by her carriage, which beamed brilliantly in the shadowy streets while making its way to the palace. Upon Cinderella's arrival at the ball, a charming gentleman (the tall, dark, and handsome type) immediately sweeps her off her feet. We know him as the prince. The lights dim, the band begins, and, the "insta-couple" waltzes from inside to out, spinning in sparkles, and gliding across bridges.[1] The prince could not be distracted from Cinderella, "so intently was he busied in gazing on her."[2] Clearly, Cinderella's heart is ruling here, and her brain has taken a backseat.

Thoughts of finally discovering love abound between the two. Whoa! Wait a second...*love*? That was fast! Of course, our romantic hearts don't want to question this evening out, but we should! Cinderella might call her flighty heart syndrome love, but it isn't. She is clearly infatuated. She is on cloud nine, but she might just want come back down to earth.

Now, it isn't bad to let your heart pound a bit after a blissful encounter with a guy. However, just because you have flutters does not mean it is love. Yes, it could be the start of something special, but it is going to take time, prayer, good judgment, and consultation with your parents and friends to figure it out. There is no need to rush.

As you get to know the person you are interested in, it is important to do a compatibility check, for emotions alone cannot rule. Get your mind in the mix with some Q and A. Do you have a similar background in terms of religion, education, and goals? Do your values match? And don't let the cuteness of your crush stop you from your querying! In the long run, these questions are very important for establishing a relationship that you won't regret. You should also observe how this person treats you. Virtue is as much a part of a romantic relationship as it is in a friendship. If this person truly loves you, their actions will reflect that love consistently.

This brings us to the question, "What is love?" In the English language, one word, *love*, describes a great many types of affection. There is love for God, love for friends, love for family, love for pets, love for food or for favorite movies, and more. However, the love that is very much anticipated by any lady is romantic love. Even though we say the word *love* with our lips, in our mind, the mystery remains. Is it a feeling? An idea? A myth? A virtue? A truth? An act? A person? Is it different for everyone? How do you know when you have found it? Well, for a basic foundation of love, let us look to the Bible.

In Scripture, we find it written, "God is love" (1 John 4:8). But still, what does that mean? We can see how God is love in an array of ways. First, as Christians, we believe in the Trinity: one God in three persons. If you think about how love works, God needs to be a community of persons because love directs itself toward *another*. Love reaches for the beloved. Therefore, "God himself is an eternal exchange of love, Father, Son, and Holy Spirit, and he has destined us to share in that exchange" (*CCC* 221). Call the Trinity a family of three. The Trinity remains a theological mystery, but by it we can see how love is the very fiber of who God is. Not only is God love, but he loves us, and calls us into that very love. "His love for his people is stronger than a mother's for her children. God loves his people more than a bridegroom his beloved" (*CCC* 219). Wow! If you thought family love was good or that romantic love was top-notch, God's love surpasses both. His amazing love should be the model for all other kinds—and it is his love that we ultimately long for in life. He is the real prince (see Isaiah 9:6), and all other loves are a mere spark compared to God's rapturous blaze. The reality is that "the heart was made for the infinite, and only the infinite can satisfy it."[3] Yet, we fool ourselves into thinking otherwise!

Ultimately, love means sacrifice. This is different than the flowery emotions we often attribute to it, but if God is love, we need to look at how he demonstrates his love. Jesus says, "Greater love has no man than this, that a man lay down his life for his friends" (John 15:13). If someone is willing to die for you, it means they prefer your life to their very own. It is the ultimate act of selflessness. By Jesus's crucifixion, he conquers sin, and wins us the victory of everlasting life. His passion on the cross is real passion, and true love. "For God so loved the world that he gave his only Son" (John 3:16).

Obviously, it is not every day that a person has the opportunity to die for his beloved. So this sacrificial love is to be demonstrated differently on a daily basis, by dying to a selfish desire, acting kindly, sharing, and so on. True love leads to loving service. There are many small ways to die to self and live for others. Someone who embraces this is precisely the kind of person you should want to date and ultimately marry. Your "someone" should have "gentleman" and "genuine" written all over him. And you too have to seek the good and to live and breathe charity by being invested in God.

Love is gift of self, not found in getting, but in giving. We can give of ourselves in many ways: give of our time and attention, affirm others, do special things for someone. True love seeks to give, not to possess a feeling, get a date, up your popularity status, fit in with your peers, get affirmed of your beauty, or acquire a first kiss. If you are looking to get something rather than give, you are probably dating for the wrong reasons.

Now the ultimate gift of self is given in the marital embrace. Keep in mind that it is only in marriage that we can give (and should give) of ourselves completely in soul and body. It is in this way that our entire self becomes a gift that is enduring. This is only possible in marriage because of a mutual vow: "to have and to hold, from this day forward, for better, for worse, for richer, for poorer, in sickness and in health, until death do us part." Before then, we must reserve the gift of our bodies—and be prudent about how much we share emotionally, as well.

Despite our culture's marketing of infidelity, you were made for but one earthly spouse, and so it is important to protect your heart so that you don't feel you have suffered several mini-divorces before the official "I do." Real love is everlasting, just like God's love for us (see Jeremiah 31:3)! Moreover, St. Paul exhorts, "Husbands, love your wives, as Christ loved the Church and gave himself up for her" (Ephesians 5:25). Once again, God is our model for love and sacrifice. Christ himself advises us to love according to his ways when he says, "Love one another as I have loved you" (John 15:12). If we take God out of the equation, we aren't talking about love, and our approach to love is all wrong.

In order to arrive upon true love, you must get to know a person. No matter how dreamy a guy is, this takes longer than one night! When Cinderella began to hurry home after hours, Prince Charming didn't even know her name. He "would give all the world to know who she was."[4] Yet, they had already exchanged a kiss and said the big *L*-word. Many of us have been equally silly, but it is time we learn. This was not love right off of the bat. You can't love someone you don't know. As you grow in knowledge of someone, then you can truly love, for real love takes deep knowledge of the beloved. This may sound rather unromantic, but in the end your prince will be everything you dreamed of if you slow your step and stay selective. It is actually more romantic to love and know someone deeply.

Let's look to the New Testament again. We read, "Love is patient and kind; love is not jealous or boastful; it is not arrogant or rude. Love does not insist on its own way; it is not irritable or resentful; it does not rejoice at wrong, but rejoices in the right. Love bears all things, believes all things, hopes all things, endures all things" (1 Corinthians 13:4–7). That's intense! Can you claim that your love is all of the above? A few things speak to me right away. This verse reaffirms that love is self-giving, and enduring. Furthermore, saying love is patient means that love takes time. It also means that love is willing to wait; therefore, someone who loves you should never pressure you or demand that you do anything that is immoral or even makes you uncomfortable. Overall, love is wanting and willing what is best for another. Love is not just a word that is said; it requires action. This verse teaches that love should be the animating force behind all that you do and all of your interactions. Once again, true love, like true friendship, is based on virtue. And friendship is also a vital base for any romantic relationship. Scripture even reminds us of this: "This is my beloved and this is my friend" (Song of Solomon 5:16).

Butterflies are fun, but they should yield to something deeper. Be selective! You can't tell an endless amount of suitors that you love them, just to move on and on and on. That, ladies, isn't love; it's recklessness.

Your heart and your ultimate match deserve more respect and care than that. It may sound cheesy, but Jesus is your ultimate Prince. You have to be content in Christ so that your heart won't roam. If you are rooted in God, he will teach you how to love and how to recognize it. Your date should also be invested in God. Excitement should not be the only thing governing your relationship decisions. Plus, dating shouldn't be a hobby, but a means of finding a husband.

So, how about the physical connection? In harmony with God's plan for you, a good phrase to keep in mind is, "Attraction does not mean action." As you acknowledge your connection growing stronger, you will probably feel drawn to express it in action. When I say "action," I don't mean holding hands or gentle kisses, but pushing physical boundaries that should be reserved for marriage. As a baptized royal princess of God, you have a vocation to chastity, and this must govern all of your romantic interactions. Therefore, you have to be careful in how you express your love for someone before you are married. Remember the above verse from Corinthians on love? It said, "Love is patient," which reminds us that anyone we date should be willing to wait until marriage for our complete gift of self. If someone wants to use you, they don't love you. In the beautiful love poetry of Songs of Solomon found in the Old Testament, wise words are shared: "I adjured you, O daughters of Jerusalem, that you stir not up nor awaken love until it please" (8:4). In other words, don't be too anxious to date, and don't mess around before you are married. Sexual union is reserved for marriage. The Church teaches in conjunction with the sixth commandment that "fornication is a carnal union between an unmarried man and an unmarried woman" (*CCC* 2353)—and that it is a sin.

Moreover, when you enter into a sexual union with someone outside of marriage, you lie with your body. Sex is the most intense body language there is. When you have sex, your body makes a promise (whether you do or not), declaring, "I am yours," even if your hearts says otherwise. Unless the "I do" has been said and you are married, there is no assurance that this is forever. Your heart won't be the same when you get it back. Once again, only in marriage are you able make a lifelong promise in body, mind, and soul—an authentic and lasting gift of self. Therefore, "let marriage be held in honor among all, and let the marriage bed be undefiled; for God will judge the immoral and adulterous" (Hebrews 13:4). Until marriage, you are simply opening yourself up to brokenness. "Sex creates a soul connection. It doesn't matter if you want it to or not. God created it that way. So the more you give sexually in a relationship, the more it rips your soul apart. It creates scars that will never go away."[5]

Our loving Father in heaven wants to protect you from hardship and harm. God intended you to become one flesh with one person only. "Therefore a man leaves his father and his mother and cleaves to his wife, and they become one flesh. And the man and his wife were both naked and were not ashamed" (Genesis 2:24–25). Marriage is for your protection so that you can make a free offering of yourself in trust and lasting fidelity, free of guilt. "When this level of intimacy is experienced within the commitments and safety of a loving marriage, it can be one of the most earthshaking and fulfilling experiences you'll ever know this side of heaven."[6] Your spouse would want you to wait.

Once you assent to this truth, it is important to set boundaries to help you accomplish purity. Your happiness and future rest on it. Remember, "a man and a woman are put in a garden on condition that they do not eat one fruit: they eat it, and lose their joy in all the fruits of the earth."[7] Learn once and for all from Adam and Eve: When God tells you not to do something, it is a good idea not to do it. He is a loving Father with your best interest in mind.

Like the Fall illustrated in Eden, fairy tales are built on terms, too. "If you really read the fairy-tales, you will observe that one idea runs from one end of them to the other—the idea that peace and happiness can only exist on some condition. This idea, which is the core of ethics, is the core of the nursery-tales. The whole happiness of fairyland hangs upon a thread, upon one thread."[8]

This is the case in our beloved Cinderella story, as well. We hear that Cinderella's evening is not everlasting. The fairy godmother says, "You must leave the ball before the clock strikes twelve. If you do not, your coach will be again become a pumpkin, your horse will be mice… while you find yourself once more in shabby clothes."[9] Like any loving guardian, the fairy godmother sets some rules. "Cinderella may have a dress woven on supernatural looms and blazing with unearthly brilliance; but she must be back when the clock strikes twelve."[10] This is her condition, or thread. Your own fairy tale and condition of happiness rests in your obedience to God's commandments; each a thread of contingency.

Cinderella shares words of obedience, but her actions speak disobedience. Our actions need to live up to our words. Before driving away, Cinderella told her godmother that she would leave the ball before midnight. Yet, despite the godmother's generosity, and Cinderella's own affirmation of the directive, she breaks the curfew. Keeping her twelve-o'clock timeline could have kept her from trouble. Instead, at the sound of the magnificent clock's final tick of twelve, Cinderella and her carriage have barely escaped the palace's closing gates. As the fairy dust fades, her ride grinds to a halt and all is transformed back to ordinary. Before the search party can find Cinderella, she scurries into the woods. Any romantic remains are trashed in the foot traffic.

If Cinderella had kept her timeline, she wouldn't be walking home in rags! Do not be ruled by impulses or excuses.

No matter how fanciful an evening out or how dreamy a date is, we must not lose sight of the wisdom outlined by our mother, the Holy Church. Just like the fairy godmother's advice to Cinderella, the Church's instructions are given to save souls from destruction, and this includes the area of chastity. St. Paul reminds us of this: "For you know what instructions we gave you through the Lord Jesus. For this is the will of God, your sanctification: that you abstain from immorality; that each of you know how to control his own body in holiness and honor, not in the passion of lust like heathen who do not know God" (1 Thessalonians 4:2–5).

As Christians, we know that we should live by the virtue of chastity. However, it is not enough to say you agree. Your actions must affirm your assertion, and there are certain measures you can and should take to help preserve your purity. It is one thing to realize why you should wait and another to understand how to wait. Learn from Cinderella: When it is time to be in bed dreaming, you should be home... alone! Obeying a curfew is just one way to guard you from temptation and mistakes. And there are many more tips to help you live out God's glorious plan for your life ahead.

Probably the most important thing you can do to help you stay pure is to pray often for the grace, desire, and strength to be chaste (even before you begin dating). Second, look for a prayerful guy who will honor you. Next, create a "won't do" list in advance for yourself, and make these boundaries specific. It is important to know that no matter how good you think a guy is, you cannot rely on the guy to set the rules or to enforce yours. "Most guys think that it's the girl's job to take control of the sex area and draw the lines. Their attitude is 'I will go as far as she will let me.' That's wrong! But that's the way our world is."[11] Unfortunately, even though guys should be strong leaders, this is one area in which they often lack leadership, so it is essential that you know that you have to be the one in control. You hold the stop sign. Never allow anyone to pressure you to push past your boundaries.

Another great idea is to go on group dates. However, if you do decide to go on a solo date, make sure you plan the date well in order to avoid boredom and downtime alone. Make sure your plan does not include going to places together where it would be easy to fall. "Danger zones are those places you will not go because chances are you'll end up doing things you should not be doing."[12] For instance, it is probably not a good idea to sit solo on a couch when you're alone, or in your dorm room when your roommate is out, or parked in an isolated area. Private environments won't aid you in the area of purity.

Clearly, the Church teaches that sex before marriage is wrong. However, that does not mean you have the liberty to do everything but have sex. If you are serious about staying pure, physical boundaries are a must for your "won't do" list. If you are wondering what you should include on your list, here are some suggestions: no passionate kissing (which means no French kissing), no kissing or touching below the chin (which means massages and tickle fights are out), no lying down together for naptime, no oral sex, and no freak dancing. Stay away from foreplay! "When it comes to love and lust, one will be in control. Either love will overpower lust and your passions will be under your control, or lust will dominate and corrupt any love that was once present. It is your choice."[13] Choose to rescue love!

Perhaps without proper insight, some of these suggestions might seem strict, overly cautious, or appear to be just another list of rules. However, I encourage you to trust wisdom instead of taking advice from the culture. The etiquette outlined above is an invitation to purity, and it is for your protection. Cinderella may not have understood the reason she had a curfew, but after she broke it she certainly did. The godmother wasn't tossing out a restriction just for the fun of it, but giving a directive for a reason. The same concept applies here. These standards of behavior are being offered to serve as a safeguard. Cinderella could have avoided calamity had she been faithful, and so can you.

In the end, love should lead to marriage because true love is tied to commitment. For that reason, the best time to think about dating is when you believe you are ready to be wed. If you are not there now, consider focusing on cultivating solid friendships with both guys and girls. When it comes to dating, it shouldn't be recreational, but purposeful. Despite a rather quick love story, I applaud the prince's understanding of this principle. His father, the king, hosts a ball for the sole purpose of helping his son find the girl of his dreams. The prince is not a player; he plans to marry Cinderella.

If you want to build a life with the man of your dreams, encourage him to act upon his love in an honorable way by pursuing you with respect. This is the way to achieve your own "happily ever after."

## Chapter Twelve

## THEIR FEET WERE TOO LARGE TO FIT
### ~ *A Smart Start to Dating* ~

One item many women can claim to collect is shoes! There is a multitude of shoe species: boots, ballet slippers, cleats, clogs, flats, flip-flops, heels, high tops, loafers, Mary Janes, moccasins, mules, platforms, pumps, sandals, slides, sling-backs, sneakers, stilettos, and more. There is just something about shoes. They take your toes on adventures, on outings, down streets and school halls, to dances, to favorite coffee shops, to winning games, on job interviews, and beyond. Shoes shuffle through the seasons, keeping your feet cozy in the cold and dashing in the dog days of summer. You could say they are always walking with you. Shoes are that fun foot accessory, coming in an array of colors and cloths, shapes and styles. Many outfits are defined by the finishing touch of the right pair of shoes.

Most likely, we have all squeezed into shoes for various reasons: Maybe we borrowed a size up or down from a friend, bought the last pair in a size that didn't quite fit, or got a great bargain on the sale rack. Yes, they might have been super cute, but in trade, we were left with blisters, Band-Aids, and cramping calves. No, despite shoes' good looks, agony is never worth it. Though ladies do not always learn, and many are willing to endure a little pain for some pretty, over and over again. Ouch! Thus, when the next posh pair is spotted, even though it doesn't quite hug your heel right, you buy it anyway, and your feet bear the wounds to prove it.

Probably the best shoe scavenge I ever had was with a friend on an excursion down to Texas. My friend Jody was on a mission for some cowboy boots. Along the way, we found a lot of charming boutiques selling boots, but nothing screamed "just right." Finding the right fit for my friend was taking a lot of time and patience. It is not every day you are in Texas (unless of course you live there), so this was the one chance to get it right! Settling was not an option. Our last stop on the map was Austin, Texas. Thankfully, we easily came across a shop filled with thousands of boots. I have never seen so many boots in one place! The aisles were filled with boots that were stacked on shelves from floor to ceiling. With what felt like a rainbow of options, Jody went to town trying all kinds of styles. At last, the perfect fit was found, and for an affordable price, too. It was almost as if that lovely pair found Jody. The mission was complete, and she had happy feet. As she continues to break in the boots, they will become branded for her feet in particular. In other words, this is a fit that will only become more fitting. Isn't that how it should be?

The classic *Cinderella* tale focuses on shoes, as well. Thanks to a fairy godmother, Cinderella's glass slippers are made to order, and so the size is perfect. This shoe does more than dancing, for it leads her back to her real fit, her husband to be (see Genesis 2:18). We all have a fit. Be it boys or boots, it is never good to force it!

While girls search for shoes, Prince Charming searches for his soul mate. He was determined to find the lovely creature who belonged to the glass slipper, and when he found her, his plan was to marry her. The morning after the ball, "folks were roused by the sound of trumpets; and through the streets of the town came the royal chamberlain, with guards and an attendant carrying the little glass slipper upon a velvet cushion."[1]

The rules are clear, but some never play by the rules, like Cinderella's stepfamily. After hearing this royal declaration, the wicked stepmother has her own declaration to make. Upon waking her daughters, who are still recovering from their fancy evening at the palace, she shares news of the proclamation. The girls' response is unenthusiastic. They don't believe they have a chance. Nevertheless, she continues to encourage her daughters, believing they could still win the prince.[2] She is scheming a squeeze into a size that isn't either of her daughters' in order to get one of them hitched to a husband who just so happens to be royalty.

Unfortunately, this aspect of the Cinderella story is not far from reality. Before we get to the important details of this fairy tale's fit forgery, let us look to history. The stepsisters are not the only collection of women who attempted to reshape their feet in order to snag a spouse. The most extreme reshaping of feet took place in China from the tenth century to the twentieth.[3] That's a thousand years of the brutal tradition called foot binding. "It was tradition. It was fashion. The men wanted it. Without bound feet, a Han Chinese girl might not get a good husband."[4] The tradition began among nobles in China, and by the seventeenth century had become the fad for all the Han Chinese citizens, who represented more than 94 percent of the population.

What exactly is foot binding? It is a technique used to reshape feet to resemble the Chinese lotus flower bud. Imagine how painful this process would have been. A well-bound foot was considered to be three inches or smaller. Foot binding began with small feet, the feet of children. Sadly, mothers encouraged the practice because they thought they were securing their daughters' future to be wed.

For the Chinese men, it was feet over face. Yet, the feet were never shown. Instead, elaborate embroidered shoes always covered them. Therefore, it was the mystery of the hidden feet that men found attractive. It was the unseen, not the seen. On the surface, foot binding appears to be all about tiny feet and amazing shoes, but the reality is that both were cultural requirements for finding a husband. In my opinion, chronic back pain and other diseases from bound feet do not seem to be a worthwhile trade. Let us steer clear of forcing a fit!

Like the Chinese mothers who encouraged their daughters to force a fit, the wicked stepmother of Cinderella does the same. With the blast of a horn, the duke arrives for the fitting, carrying the prized slipper upon a purple pillow, and the stepsisters have set the scene. The pressure is high from their mother, who demands that they don't fail her. In order to catch a companion, both daughters are determined to fool him into thinking they have the feet that fit. As they welcome their Imperial Grace, they attempt to act with grace, but their uncouth nature cannot be hidden. The duke begins to read the proclamation, and before he can finish, in a bickering manner, the two girls make empty claims of slipper ownership. "Cinderella's stepsisters were desperate to try on the slipper. But, though they pinched their toes and squeezed their heels their feet were far too large to fit into it."[5]

Overall, the stepsisters' attempt is pretty ridiculous, especially because we know the slipper's true owner and how the story ends. However, when it comes to you, you do not yet know how your story ends or who your prince is. In the process of awaiting him, how many fits will you force? It is important to know your shoe size, and what style you like. If you do not know what kind of girl you are, you won't know what you are looking for in a guy. Get to know yourself first! That way, when you find the wrong fit, you will be able to spot it. And when you find the right fit, you will be prepared to make a true gift of yourself because you possess yourself. You cannot give what you do not have, and you won't find yourself in someone else.

Do not make the same mistake with guys as you do with your feet. There are certain shoes, and certain types of guys, that you should avoid. Some combinations just do not make for a good pair. Take a look.

1. **The starter heel:** Remember these? Yours were probably pink with a square toe and heel no taller than an inch. You may have prized them when you were ten, but you wouldn't be caught dead in them now. Why? They are a "practice heel." Such starter heels lack the sophistication that you and your feet really desire. These shoes just won't see you through your journey. What kind of relationship does the starter heel resemble? The first guy or two that you date. You are excited about them at the time, but know deep down in your heart that they are not the kind of guy you really want to end up with permanently. This kind of relationship should end swiftly, but sometimes you justify these relationships on the grounds that they are about practicing for the real prince, and you stay in the relationships too long. Shoes may be something to practice with, but people are not! Boys are not objects, and they aren't for your use. If he is not the one, it is time to get back to a single status. If you are honest with yourself, this concept of "practice" relationships is a bit absurd. After all, do you need to practice to be a best friend with someone else?

2. **The thrift-store rescue:** I am a fan of thrift-store finds, but thrift-store rescues are in a different category. These are pairs of shoes that have no business being placed on the rack before a trip to the shoemaker.

Picture it: The shoes appear to be cute, but the heels are worn down, the soles have no grip, and the interior is ripped. They need some major doctoring! Yet, you see them and are convinced you can fix them up to quality shoe standards. Therefore, the pair is purchased. And instead of sending them to the shoe repairman, you begin the undertaking on your own. Be it shoes or men, I like to call such an attempt the "savior syndrome." Like the thrift-store rescue, this type of guy is attractive, but he is emotionally broken and needs help. You believe you can help him, change him, and be there for him. It is true we can support and care for our friends, but there is a lot of work that belongs to the soul-maker, God. If we really want to help someone, we should lead him to Christ instead of trying to personally fix his issues ourselves. Keep in mind that man and woman come together to serve the Lord in one another and others, not to be each other's savior! Such a man owes it to you to spend quality time with Christ working through his wounds, healing, and growing in strength before getting involved romantically. Otherwise, he is simply falsely advertising himself. No matter how he markets himself, he is not for sale! Don't force a fit with a fixer-upper!

3. **The sneaker:** Looking for something comfortable? You have found the right shoe! This is the shoe that will see you through all that walking you need to do, but it may look very out of place at a fancy dinner, Church, or on your wedding day (just to name a few). Sneakers might be comfortable, but they aren't exciting, and they are not suited for certain events. Furthermore, sneakers are the shoes your feet settle for when in reality they would rather be in a pair of cute sandals or heels. In the same way, there are certain guys out there that you feel very comfortable with, but your connection and conversations lack sparks. You lack true compatibility. Your day-to-day interactions are flat, and deep down you feel that this isn't the right guy for you. You

sense you are settling, but because the relationship is comfortable, it is easy to keep walking with it instead of breaking it off. There is nothing horrible about this guy, but there really isn't anything great about him, either. He gets an overall "OK" rating. He's just not quite what your heart is longing for in a spouse. This type of relationship can make your passions and gifts wither. Being comfortable in a relationship is good, but settling is not. There are plenty of other comfortable, yet versatile, fits out there.

4. **The sky-high stiletto:** This sleek shoe is quite attractive, but after a trek in these towering heels your legs and feet will have terrible pain! In fact, stiletto high heels take their name from the stiletto knife or dagger, which has a long slender blade and comes to a thin point. Thus, strolling in these skyscrapers goes beyond walking on pins and needles. Despite this shoe's good looks, it was named after a weapon! In a similar way, a guy might be very handsome, but if he carries with him a bad reputation and treats you poorly, striding with him will cause you pain. A guy who entertains bad behavior, such as lying, cheating, drinking, doing drugs, neglecting responsibilities, getting bad grades, or pushing for promiscuity, is not a fit. You have no business even entertaining him as a possible husband.

5. **The flip-flop:** These shoes are great for the beach and preserving your pedicure. However, once you have gone several miles on the board-walk, your feet come to realize that they were lacking quality support. In addition, you might quickly be tired of their echoing "flip-flop" sound. These puppies simply can't go the distance. When it comes to the guy department, the one who can be described as a flip-flop is one who does not support you. His lack of support can come in a variety of forms, including poor leadership, fiscal irresponsibility, inattentiveness to what's important to you, a lack of plans for his future, a lukewarm

faith or none at all, and an absence of virtue. He is just not strong. He can't support himself, and he definitely can't support you. Moreover, the flip-flopper lacks consistency. One moment he is charming, but the next he is cranky and careless. Eventually, his selfishness will shine through to you. It may start out wonderfully, but strolling with this guy will reveal his true identity. He is more of a burden than a blessing. Do not bother with this floppy fit.

6. **The trendy shoe:** Kicks that are the must-have shoe own the "trendy" title. If your feet aren't covered in chic, you might feel shy. It is OK to stand solo and be confident. This principle stands for boyfriends, too. Just because everyone else has someone, doesn't mean you should force a fit in order to fit in with the crowd. Perhaps you justify grabbing up any guy because you are sick of waiting for your special someone, or you simply think it's time you had a boyfriend. It is important to consult God before you grab an apple (see Genesis 3) or a guy that doesn't belong to you. Finding someone to be a pair with you will take patience. Don't just be trendy; be open to God's possibilities and timing instead.

7. **The platform:** How's the weather up there? When you put on these high-rise shoes, you appear to have grown half a foot overnight. Nevertheless, it is a façade. You are posing as something you are not, someone who is six inches taller! In the case of accessorizing, shoes that make you beanstalk height might be harmless, but boys who change you are not. You should never continue dating someone who makes you feel like you have to be someone else. If you don't feel like you can be yourself, then the fit is all wrong.

Outside of shoes, there are many other reasons not to force a fit. You shouldn't date someone because you are lonely, feel desperate, desire to make someone else jealous, or feel it is time you had your first kiss.

Also, you should not date a feeling. You date people, not emotions. If you are in love with love, and not a person, it is time to admit it.

It is important to try on shoes and spend some time walking in them instead of relying on the size listed. Go on dates and get to know someone before things turn into a long relationship. If a pair of shoes or a date don't fit right, then don't commit to them. When you force a fit, you are preventing true matches. If you have discerned that you are not called to marry the person you are dating, it is time to say goodbye. You have just determined that this is not your *sole* mate, and so you have yet to meet your prince. You are also keeping him from the spouse God intends for him. It is good to admit it if the prince belongs to someone else (or that he is not a prince at all), and in the right time, yours will be revealed to you. I am sure Cinderella would have appreciated such a gesture from her stepsisters. Let God set you up!

## Chapter Thirteen

### HERE IS THE PRINCE'S FUTURE BRIDE
*~ Brides to Be ~*

There is a point in most every girl's life, as she grows in age and maturity, when she starts to get "itchy bride" symptoms. Steadily, thoughts of being a bride consumer her. She begins to daydream about her wedding day—that special event filled with "something old, something new, something borrowed, and something blue."

As I began to sense that I'd like to hear wedding bells in my future, something really special happened. At a family reunion, months after the passing of my maternal grandmother, my aunt revealed that her old wedding dress had been found. She brought out the simple box it had been stored in for more than sixty years! It stood as an icon of the marital longevity shared by my grandparents.

Together, we slowly unwrapped the treasure and found the vintage dress to be in amazing condition. I sensed that all family members' eyes were on me. Everyone seemed to have the same idea, which was for me to try it on. I was excited, but unsure if it would even be my size. Remarkably, it fit! This 1940s dress was designed quite stylishly for its time, with an empire waist and sheer fabric that went from the neck to the sleeves, which sat off the shoulders a bit. The dress was incredibly made with beautiful satiny fabric, beadwork, a long train, and a trail of buttons down the back. It felt good to be in a wedding dress and to think forward to the day when I would one day be married. As the tradition goes, I had my *something old*. On a woman's wedding day, this old item is a symbol of the continuity a bride has with her family and her past.

Later that year, another surprise occurred. I received a small package from one my mother's friends, a sweet woman in her eighties named Polly. Enclosed in the parcel was a collection of handmade handkerchiefs. The note read: *I have treasured these for many years. With love I am sending them for future use on your wedding day to be your something blue. Hopefully you will cherish it as I have.* The note went on to share about the Polish woman who had made the handkerchiefs and the stories that they held. The dear woman's letter to me ended with: *Remember me on your wedding day with a little prayer.* I felt so preciously remembered and encouraged. Indeed, I had my *something blue*. This links a bride with an old tradition because, surprisingly, before the late nineteenth century, blue, not white, was the wedding dress color of choice. It symbolized love, modesty, and fidelity. Of course, blue is often associated with Our Lady.

Bridal bliss was beckoning me, but I still needed *something new* (to symbolize the optimism and hope of the bride's new life), *something borrowed*, (to remind a bride that she can depend on the mentorship and support of friends and family), and of course I was in need of a bridegroom! Obviously, that last one was in God's hands. Nevertheless, my job was to discern carefully what kind of bride he was calling me to be. God's call is exactly what a vocation is all about. In fact, the word *vocation* comes from the Latin word *vocare*, which means "to call." At the heart of this call is the reality that we are all brides and brides-to-be.

How are we already brides? Every baptized member of the Church is part of the one body, and that body is considered to be the very bride of Christ. This bridal understanding is not a generic attribution, but rather extends intimately to every individual within it. "The apostles speak of the whole Church and of each of the faithful, members of his Body, as a bride 'betrothed' to Christ the Lord so as to become one spirit with him" (*CCC* 796). This insight is declared throughout the Scriptures by many of the Old Testament prophets, Gospel parables, St. Paul's letters, and in the book of Revelation. For instance, in the book of Isaiah, we read, "For your Maker is your husband" (54:5).

As seen, every Church member carries the title of "bride" already, but every lady, by the nature of her vocation, is still a bride-*to-be*. Usually, the word *bride* instantly calls to mind a woman marrying a man. However, this is not the only bridal reality. Religious sisters, nuns, and consecrated women are also brides. St. John Paul II wrote: "A woman is 'married' either through the sacrament of marriage or spiritually through marriage to Christ. *In both cases marriage* signifies the 'sincere gift of the person' of the bride to the groom."[1] Perhaps being "married to Christ" sounds strange, but ultimately a deep love for Christ will awaken this desire within a woman if religious life is her true call. Likewise, a true love for Christ will also help those called to marriage to be faithful to Jesus in their vocations. On your wedding day, you will happily embrace your bridegroom, whoever he is!

In *Cinderella*, as Cinderella arrives at the ball, the duke is privately sharing a romantic possibility for the prince to the king. As our vision is filled with Cinderella's beauty, the line he speaks seems to foreshadow her future. He says, "Here is the Prince's future bride."[2] Cinderella does not yet know what kind of bride she will be, but we do, thanks to this clue. In our own call to be brides, all of us are destined for royalty, as well.

Break out the crown, bride-to-be! Royalty is God's desire for each one of his daughters. In fact, in Jewish tradition, the bride and her bridegroom were called a king and queen on their wedding day. Along with the Orthodox, some Catholic rites continue in this tradition today, particularly the Eastern rites, such as Melkite and Byzantine. This custom known as "the crowning" takes place within the sacrament of marriage. First, a ribbon is tied on the crowns to symbolize the couple's unity. Next, the crowns are placed on their heads prayerfully in the name of the Father, of the Son, and Holy Spirit in order to express the sign of God's blessing upon them. The crowns symbolize three things. One: The Crowns of Royalty represent the kingship they have over their new family, for they are called to rule their home with wisdom, justice, and integrity. Two: The Crowns of Martyrdom remind them to reflect God's love in their own marriage through their mutual sufferings, joys, and love. Three: The Crowns of Kingdom remind the couple that their marriage must be centered on the kingdom of God. You won't be any less royal if you are called to a spiritual marriage through religious life. All that sisters do, they do for the sake of the kingdom of heaven. Their life of prayer, sacrifice, and loving service is all for the glory of the King. Together, all brides pray, "Thy Kingdom Come, Thy will be done."

There are a great many similarities between sisters and nuns and laywomen brides. Personally, I always thought the two bridal callings were starkly different, but they are not. Let's begin with the dress. Women called to traditional marriage will wear a wedding dress for the big day. Religious sisters visually preach being a bride, as well, for they wear their wedding dress perpetually! For example, the Dominican Sisters of Nashville wear a white habit, along with a veil that can be either white or black. Sound familiar? It reminds me of what most laywomen brides wear to walk down the aisle.

Of course a religious sister's attire differs from order to order. Some wear brown, blue, or black. The Holy Spirit Adoration Sisters even go pretty in pink, with their rose-colored habits standing as a symbol of joy![3] Whatever color, consecrated sisters dress in this way in order to manifest that they are indeed brides of Christ. Not only do sisters dress their body, they also dress their hearts. In many orders, such as the Dominicans, each piece of the habit has a short prayer that is associated with it. Therefore, as a nun gets dressed, she prays the prayer that is affiliated with each garment. She is dressing her mind and body in a bridal reality.

Bridal commonalities between laywomen and religious are not just in the fabric; they are also in the facts. Outside of the wardrobe, the first connection is that both brides take vows. These vows are to one spouse, and one spouse only. For laywomen, this spouse is a layman, but for religious sisters, their spouse is Christ. Sisters are "betrothed mystically to Christ, the Son of God, and are dedicated to the service of the Church" (*CCC* 923). Though both brides take vows, religious sisters take more than one. Before a sister takes her final vow, she will have passed through different stages and spent years discerning.

The first part of discernment is called *postulancy*, which is the first year following a young woman's entrance into a religious community. During this time, she is able to get to know the community, and the community becomes acquainted with her. In a way, it is similar to a girl and a guy beginning a friendship. At the end of this period, she receives a habit. Next comes the *novitiate*, which usually lasts two years. Perhaps, this stage is comparable to a guy and girl courting. Upon the conclusion of this chapter, if both the sister and the order discern that religious life is God's will for her, she makes a series of vows (chastity, poverty, and obedience) for a period of three years. Once the three years have transpired, the sister makes a *temporary profession* for another two years. This is akin to engagement. Overall, a sister will have made temporary vows for at least five years before expressing her commitment with a *final vow*, which is made at a Mass of Profession. Therefore, entering religious life is a careful discernment process—just like marriage. Once a final vow is made, the state of life, be it marriage or consecrated life, is considered permanent. Women of both vocations express their "I am taken" status outwardly by wearing a ring.

Once a vow has been made in marriage or religious life, it requires complete fidelity of mind, body, and soul. However, just because a woman is betrothed does not mean she becomes blind and never again recognizes a handsome man. She is, however, intentional by constantly directing her love to her spouse alone. Despite any attraction that comes, she must be firm in her fidelity for the spouse she has chosen, be it a man or the Son of Man, Jesus.

This commitment manifests itself through the virtue of chastity. Most obviously, chastity is a part of religious life. "From apostolic times, Christian virgins, called by the Lord to cling only to him with greater freedom of heart, body, and spirit have decided with the Church's approval to live in the respective states of virginity or perpetual chastity for 'the sake of the kingdom of heaven'" (*CCC* 923). Thus, religious sisters refrain from any sexual expression of love because they are to remain a sign of the Church's love for Christ (see *CCC* 922).

However, chastity is not just for religious. Surprise! Though married women are not called to a life of virginity, they are still called to chastity within marriage. This is called conjugal chastity, and it is practiced through a couple's actions and mutual fidelity. Chastity encourages joint respect of each other's dignity and forbids adultery and other unnatural sexual activity, including the use of contraception. In marriage, the use of Natural Family Planning will also call a couple into periods of abstinence. Overall, "people should cultivate chastity in the way that is suited to their state of life. Some profess virginity or consecrated celibacy, which enables them to give themselves to God alone with an undivided heart in a remarkable manner, others live in the way prescribed for all by moral law, whether they are married or single" (*CCC* 2349).

Ultimately, brides become one body with their spouse. Genesis reminds us that in the consummation of marriage, "[the two] become one flesh" (Genesis 2:24). In a mystical manner, the Church, the bride of Christ, also becomes one body with Christ. This is most clearly seen in Holy Communion. In the Eucharist, Jesus is truly made real (see John 6:52–55). When the consecrated host is consumed, a person is consuming the Body, Blood, Soul, and Divinity of Christ into her body. Through this mystery, as a baptized Catholic, Christ's very Body enters our own body, and we are personally united to him, both spiritually and physically. "He who eats my flesh and drinks my blood abides in me, and I in him" (John 6:56). This holy union is not just reserved for religious sisters, but all of the Church members who approach the altar of the Lord during the Mass. Therefore, religious sisters are also made one with Christ in a spiritual way. "[She] who is united to the Lord becomes one spirit with him" (1 Corinthians 6:17).

Another way that religious life and marriage are connected is through motherhood. Both vocations are called to be fruitful, but this will be reflected differently in each. Without a doubt, motherhood is intimately tied to marriage. "By its very nature, the institution of marriage and married love is ordered to the procreation and education of offspring, and it is in them that it finds its crowning glory."[4] A mother must attend to not only the body but also to each child's soul.

In the process of educating children, a mother is called to raise her kids with faith in Christ Jesus. Though religious sisters are not called to be physical mothers, they are called to spiritual motherhood. This type of motherhood "can express itself as concern for people, especially the most needy: the sick, the handicapped, the abandoned, orphans, the elderly, children, young people, the imprisoned and, in general, people on the edges of society."[5] In fact, spiritual motherhood allows for great generosity, since it extends to the entire human race. This spiritual motherhood is centered on winning souls for Christ.

Entering into a vocation is a life-changing experience. This is symbolized in the fact that, with both consecrated life and marriage, a woman is invited to change her name. Virginal brides often take on new first names, and lay brides lay down their last name for their husband's surname. Why does this matter? Throughout the old and new covenants, a name change always accompanied a transformation; it signified a change of identity. For instance, Abram, which means "high father" was given the name "Abraham" by God, which means "father of multitude." His wife's name was changed from "Sarai," meaning "my princess" to "Sarah," which is defined as "mother of nations." These names are definitely appropriate for this couple's mission because, as promised by God the Father, many generations would flow from their union. In the New Testament, before St. Peter was given the title "the rock," as Jesus commissioned him to feed his sheep as the first pope, he was known as Simon. In a similar way, before St. Paul had a major revamping of faith, he was called Saul. He went from persecuting Christians to one amazing evangelizer, and his name reflected that. Names express new life and new possibilities in the light of Christ. A vocation is truly life-altering, and so it is very appropriate that it would be accompanied by a name change.

It is clear that Jesus held marriage in high esteem. In fact, Christ's very first miracle was at a wedding, the wedding feast at Cana in Galilee (see John 2:1–11). When Our Lady takes note that the newlyweds have run out of wine, she prompts her Son into action. Jesus turns six huge jars of water into six jars of wine. (Ultimately, this foreshadows Jesus turning wine into his blood on the night before his crucifixion at Passover.) The miracle alone is awe-inspiring, but two important verses stand out in particular. First, in order for this miracle to occur, those involved had to take clear direction from Christ. Therefore, Mary instructs those involved to, "Do whatever he tells you" (John 2:5). She is speaking to us, too. As brides in the making, each lady should do whatever Christ tells her. Turning to Christ, seeking his will, and following his call will lead every young woman to her vocation.

It is also important to emphasis this verse from the wedding scene in Cana: "Every man serves the good wine first; and when men have drunk freely, then the poor wine; but you have kept the good wine until now" (John 2:10). Jesus saves the best for last! If your bridal clock is already ticking away, keep in mind that it might be awhile before Prince Charming shows up. Nevertheless, if you put the wine selection—or spouse selection—in Christ's hands, it will be better than you can imagine. Trust in the Lord. Waiting for Christ's best takes time and patience, but it is always worth it.

In the meantime, make sure you are serious about your bridal preparations. As you wait upon the Lord to direct you to the type of bride you will be, stay true to your spouse by being chaste. Every bride should wear white for a reason, to reflect her purity. As you discern, pray for your future husband, perhaps by lifting him up as your main Mass intention every time you attend the sacred liturgy. The Mass is the highest form of prayer, and you can bring your personal intentions there and mentally lay them before the altar. Over the years, you will accumulate a lot of prayers for your spouse-to-be, which is extremely important. These prayers will yield great fruit in his life and in your marriage. If you are called to be a virginal bride, your prayers will not be wasted. They will be poured out for the Church, which contains many souls in need of prayers.

Most important, it is not enough to merely ponder your vocation; you must pray about it. Pray for guidance and that your heart is open to God's will. Also, make an effort to meet some religious sisters by visiting different orders. Too often, young women are isolated from religious communities and never given the opportunity to meet these women of God. You will be pleasantly surprised by the amount of beauty, joy, and zeal that is found in the consecrated life. Every young woman who is truly serious about her faith, and in love with Jesus, should at least consider the religious life in the quiet of her heart. God will lead you toward the vocation that will answer your prayers. Whatever your call, you will be a beautiful bride called out of "cinder" to splendor.

# Part Three

• ~ • ~ •

SLEEPING BEAUTY
"The King's daughter shall in her fifteenth year
prick herself with a spindle…"[1]
—*The Brothers Grimm*

• ~ • ~ •

## Chapter Fourteen

### I WILL TURN HER INTO A FLOWER
#### ~ *Seasons of Fulfillment* ~

E very year is marked by seasons. Some places experience what they call a "dry season" and a "wet season." However, many encounter the traditional four: summer, fall, winter, and spring. Each season has its own character and brings with it a unique ambiance. Our lives are very much shaped by the seasons in what we wear, what we do, and even what we eat. With each stretch come aspects that I am eager to enjoy and other elements that I begrudgingly endure.

I live in the Northeast, and when summer comes around, I bask in the beauty of the bright sun that wakes early and goes to bed late. I love cool refreshing drinks and licking frosty ice cream from crunchy cones. All of the fruits and flavors of summer are scrumptious. Visits to the beach or pool are a nice way to cool down, too. Nights filled with the cadence of crickets and the disco lights of fireflies are soothing to the soul. Yet the summer heat and thick air caused by humidity, found in the east, can be brutal. That's summer's strike!

Sunny days seem to fade into fall, which delivers its own brightness in a vast array of colors hanging from branches. Hikes, hayrides, crunchy leaves beneath your feet, corn mazes, bonfires, orchard outings, spicy smells, a collection of pies, and hot cider, are some of fall's many pleasures. Amusements aside, autumn carries a threat: the warning of stark days ahead. Fall fades slowly, as the trees shed, the sky darkens, and the crisp air is heightened to cold. With fall's distractions, winter's arrival is sneaky.

If I could skip winter in the Northeast, I would. Honestly, I am plagued by its duration. Somehow it feels longer than all the other seasons. It is down-to-the-bones cold and continually cloudy, and the days are much abbreviated. In life, some spans of time are just more difficult to sustain than others. But, despite my distaste for winter, I can still find goodness in it. Snow is beautiful and brings with it opportunities that include front-yard snowmen, homemade igloos, snow angels, snowball fights, sledding, skiing, and ice skating. When you retreat inside from the icy outdoors, it is undeniably nice to cuddle up by the fireplace with a snuggly blanket and hot chocolate filled with mini marshmallows. The season's hearty comfort foods served are delightful too, be it silky thick soups, crusty breads, velvety mashed potatoes, tender roasts, gooey mac-and-cheese, steamy potpies, or fresh-baked anything!

Each year, once I begin to believe that winter will never end, spring thankfully arrives with sprouts of new life. The world is once again resurrected from days of hibernation. Song birds sing, bees buzz, butterflies flutter, and flowers bud and bloom. It is a glorious crescendo! Trees appear lacy, and the ground is covered in pastel rainbows, as flowers appear in symphonic style. When the inevitable rain appears, umbrellas pop, and polka-dot rain boots stomp through puddles. I do like spring, but its slow beginnings make me impatient, and I've never been a fan of rain (even if you get to wear cute apparel).

Seasons are not limited to the sun's orbit around earth. As Scripture says, "For everything there is a season, and a time for every matter under heaven: a time to be born, and a time to die; / a time to plant, and a time to pluck up what is planted" (Ecclesiastes 3:1–2). Each day is filled with seasons: morning, afternoon, and night, (found to be) rainy or bright. School is filled with seasons: semesters, homecoming and prom, exams, homework highs and lows, sport seasons, and holiday vacations. As Catholics, we recognize the seasons in the liturgical calendar, which include Advent, Christmas, Ordinary Time, Lent,[1] and Easter. Even our lives are filled with seasons: infancy, childhood, adolescence, the young adult years, and beyond. More specifically, the very life of a woman is seasonal: singleness, betrothal, marriage, and motherhood (God willing!). Seasons are also reflected by a woman's body, changing from square to shapely, the arrival of an ongoing monthly menstrual cycle, pregnancy, and later menopause. Like weather intervals, every season in a woman's life and experienced by the body will come with a variety of expectations, emotions, joys, displeasures, and challenges. Seasons turn in time and at a different pace for all women. The fact that women are seasonal must not be ignored. Instead, keeping the seasons in mind will help direct every woman's life, just like the weather report guides a lady's choice in apparel.

One lady, a princess actually, that we have the privilege of seeing through some seasons is Sleeping Beauty. We can learn a lot from her. Here is a summary of her initial season: After a long-awaited arrival, she is born into royalty and named Aurora, after the dawn. At the kingdom's celebration, the tiny princess is welcomed with gifts from three good fairies named Flora, Fauna, and Merryweather. The first two share gifts of beauty and song, but before the third good fairy can share her particular offering, the scene goes from gleeful to grim. Maleficent, the evil fairy, arrives uninvited. She hatefully bequeaths a "gift" of her own, declaring that on the princess's fifteenth birthday, Aurora will

prick her finger and die. Horror fills the kingdom. The blow is soft-
ened by the last good fairy's gift, which turns the spell from one of
death to one of sleep. True love's kiss is the antidote. Nevertheless, this
is one anticipated dark season that all hope the princess will never face.

The three good fairies shrink in size to brainstorm ideas for
concealing the princess from the enemy. Almost instantly, Flora excit-
edly concludes to change the princess into a flower because she could
not prick her finger in such a form. Fauna agrees that she would be
a beautiful flower. Merryweather speaks some sense to both fairies,
sharing that Maleficent may send a frost. After dismissing this faulty
plan, Flora decides on a new one: to raise the princess in the abandoned woodcutter's cottage deep in the forest. And to dodge suspicion,
the three decide to bring Aurora up free of magic, forgoing their wings
and wands. Upon the king and queen's heavy-hearted approval, Aurora
goes from princess to peasant. Though she does not appear as a flower,
her new guardians give her the name of one, calling her Briar Rose.
Therefore, the blonde beauty will blossom through several seasons of
her life as a rustic rose, hidden away in the woods.[2]

Like Briar Rose, we can also view ourselves as flowers. Like women,
flowers enjoy seasons: budding, blooming, and eventually folding to a
finish. In fact, such a metaphor is even found in Scripture. In the Song
of Solomon, a maiden declares, "I am a rose of Sharon, a lily of the
valleys" (2:1). St. Therese of Lisieux, known as the "Little Flower," also
sees souls as flowers:

> All the flowers he has created are beautiful, how the splendor
> of the rose and the whiteness of the lily do not take away
> the perfume of the little violet or the delightful simplicity of
> the daisy. I understood that if all flowers wanted to be roses,
> nature would lose her springtime beauty, and the fields would

no longer be decked out with little wild flowers. And so it is in the world of souls, Jesus's garden. He willed to create great souls comparable to lilies and roses, but he has created smaller ones and these must be content to be daises or violets destined to give joy to God's glances when he looks down at his feet. Perfection consists in doing his will, in being what he wills us to be.[3]

Indeed, it is the desire of God that you live the seasons established by your body, emotions, and life's course with authentic femininity in mind. He has willed you to be a woman.

As a flowering woman, the first season a lady will walk is the season of becoming. This seed time or sowing period allows a girl to become a young woman, and from there, an adult. It is a season of self-realization; a time where you discover the ins and outs of who you are, how you best express yourself, what you like, what your interests and gifts are, and most important, who God is calling you to be. It is truly a time to grow.

A lot must take place before a posy reaches its prime. Like the underground formation of flowers and Sleeping Beauty, this season may require that you are hidden for a while. A long-standing tradition that began in Europe is to present young women to society at a formal debut or debutante ball. The original purpose for this event was to announce that a young woman was eligible to marry. Thus, until this formal announcement, young women were hidden from suitors.

Even in today's world, this season is a must in order to properly prepare for the crown that marks your mission, as well as your prince's arrival. Like my itch for the end of winter, it is not always easy to wait for the prince. The length of this season will vary. Therefore, do not waste time counting the length of another lady in waiting's season. Nevertheless, it is important to see this season as a gift—a time that allows you to study something you are passionate about, become involved in activities, take on hobbies, go on adventures, and to enjoy time with your girlfriends. All of these things are much-needed fertilizer, which helps you flourish and figure out the kind of flower that you are. If you live your life to the fullest in your single years, you will not feel like you are missing out on anything when the God-appointed time comes for marriage and motherhood. Instead, your heart will be ready to give fully to your husband and children, knowing that you are entering into a different kind of adventure.

Whatever state of life God is drawing you to, be it marriage or religious life, it is vital to keep his call in mind in order to plan accordingly. One season lends itself to the next. For example, when it comes to clothes, fall fashions are brought into stores well before summer's end. Though you can still sport summer clothes, you just might make a purchase to add to your upcoming autumn wardrobe. It is a time of preparation. Every gal should be sure to have the right garments come the first frost, or she will suffer shivers. While living fully every season, it is also good to anticipate the next, so you won't be blindsided when it arrives.

This advice doesn't just apply to fashion. In God's goodness and divine wisdom, there is a time of transition built into all seasons, including those of a woman's life. Slow seasonal shifts allow a woman to prepare her heart for the upcoming changes. Two big examples of interims include the six-month engagement required by the Church before marriage and the nine months of pregnancy before the arrival of a child. Such periods of adaptation truly allow a woman to prepare for the new and major changes ahead. All seasonal life changes will require some adjusting, so it is important to plan for them, pray through them, and ask for the grace to accept them.

In particular, I want to address how to plan ahead for one particular state of life, the season of marriage, because most women will be called to this vocation. What I am about to share, society won't tell you. In fact, it will misguide you. We must choose to either be catechized by the culture or by the Church, for an attempt to follow both will leave you confused. One thing is sure; God has a mission in mind for you. Chapter four spoke of the three-fold reality of vocation: primary vocation (baptized Christian), personal vocation (occupation), and state of life (marriage, religious, etc.). A person's vocation is made manifest through all those dimensions.

How good it is to have women contributing to society through their vocations! Pope John Paul II thought so, too, and wrote to women telling them so in his "Letter to Women." He thanked daughters, sisters, wives, mothers, religious sisters, and working women with equal gratitude. To those with a career, he said: "Thank you, *women who work!* You are present and active in every area of life—social, economic, cultural, artistic, and political. In this way you make an indispensable contribution to the growth of a culture which unites reason and feeling, to a model of life ever open to the sense of 'mystery,' to the establishment of economic and political structures ever more worthy of humanity."[4] There is no doubt that women have many gifts to share through work. However, it is very important that work does not prevent a woman from authentically living out the other aspects of her vocation. Therefore, if you feel called to marriage, you must approach the selection of your career with care. Marriage brings with it responsibilities. In particular, you must be open to life in your marriage, and as a woman this should be a key part of your discernment in your job choice. In fact, the very word *matrimony*, which comes from Latin, reveals this very mission. *Mater* means "mother," and the suffix *monia* refers to "action, state, or condition." Therefore, the word explicitly means "the establishment of a mother."⁵ To my surprise, children even understand the connection between marriage and children. The morning after my wedding, a five-year-old girl guest approached me at brunch, and while pointing to my belly asked, "Is there a baby in there?" My face flushed a little, but in the end I was thankful for the assumption that marriage (even one under twenty-four-hours old) should beget babies. Society has a lot to learn from God's little ones!

As a flower, you are called to bear fruit in your marriage. Just as St. Elizabeth declared to Mary, "Blessed is the fruit of your womb" (Luke 1:42), so is yours. In creation, all fruit begins with a flower. Strawberries begin with delicate white blooms, tomatoes from yellow florets, and apples from pink blossoms. The metamorphosis is quite a mysterious process. Even more so is a "seed" growing into a child within a woman's womb. It's a miracle worth fathoming, for life is literally blossoming inside a woman's body. With God's grace and the help of a man, the female body is capable of building a person. A woman simply needs to sleep and eat, and the body does all the rest. Wow! How crazy is that? This special privilege, given to women alone, should be honored. Until a woman experiences pregnancy, especially the feeling of life within her as the baby kicks and moves, the delight cannot be grasped.

However, in today's age, society often depicts children as career destroyers, encouraging only a tidy family of two—or eliminating them altogether with the pill or abortion. Society wants you to appear more as a man than a woman, and that means rejecting who you were made to be, including your fertility. Yet Christ says, "Let the children come to me, and do not hinder them" (Matthew 19:14). Children are blessings, not curses. Several seasons ago, you were once a child, too. How wonderful that your mother gave you life!

So as long as marriage is on your mind, it is wise to select a profession that is compatible with being a wife and mother, even before you are actively serving in either role. That way you won't have to feel like you are choosing between the two later. It is smart seasonal foresight! As a woman, your body is stamped with the mission to conceive and bear children. In no way does the Church say a woman should not work outside of the home. However, if you have to use contraception in order to maintain a position in your field, it is not what God is calling you to (see chapter eight).

Some seasons of your life may enable you to work full-time, while others may require you to work part-time or perhaps only at home. In planning ahead, it is worthwhile to pick an occupation that will offer some flexibility in your schedule and location. There are so many options! In a vocation to marriage, creativity is key in order to express your talents both in the home and outside of it. For a timeless example of a woman in economic pursuit from her home, read Proverbs 31.

Despite culture's emphasis on work outside of the home, it is also not the most important thing a woman can do with her life. In the collective years of life, the childbearing season is short. It is important to note that at the end of time, all that you have created and undertaken will cease, except for your children. "One day, all human accomplishments will be reduced to a pile of ashes. But every single child to whom a woman has given birth will live forever, for he has been given an immortal soul made to God's image and likeness."[6] Women can only bear children for a season, and it is clearly an unparalleled eternal mission, one to be cherished. Therefore, during this season of active motherhood, a woman should seek a special dedication to her children. The trend of the time is to outsource the responsibility of motherhood by way of daycare, nannies, or grandparents. But should a woman forgo precious moments with her children for her career?

Society has trained women to think that their value is caught up in having a career outside of the home. There is an intense whisper that says that staying home and caring for your children is something you should be embarrassed to do. Childrearing is considered to be a less important mission than work outside the home, something to outsource, or even a worthless endeavor. Pope John Paul II noticed this trend, too, and said: "The mentality which honors women more for their work outside the home than for their work within the family must be overcome. This requires that men should truly esteem and love women with total respect for their personal dignity, and that society should create and develop conditions favoring work in the home."[7] Nurturing a family with an undivided heart is the most special and important thing a woman can do!

In God's eyes, your vocation (or state of life) to the married life outranks your career or personal vocation. Edith Stein (St. Teresa Benedicta of the Cross) had a great amount of wisdom to share on the topic of women and work. She said, "Any social condition is an unhealthy one which compels married women to seek gainful employment and makes it impossible for them to manage their home. And we should accept as normal that the married woman is restricted to domestic life at a time when her household duties exact her total energies."[8] Thus, a woman needs to dedicate herself to her primary vocation, but as the demands of her household and family engagements lessen, she may open herself more to working outside of the home (or perhaps from home). In other words, Edith Stein is promoting seasons of fulfillment.

Edith Stein clearly recognizes the supreme order of vocational duties; however, she acknowledges that at times women may feel called to share their gifts outside of the home, as well. In fact, she encourages that they do. She shares, "Wherever the circle of domestic duties is too narrow for the wife to attain the full formation of her powers, both nature and reason concur that she reach out beyond this circle."[9] It is good for women to make contributions to society through a job, volunteering, or in some other capacity. In fact, taking time away from the home can be a means of rejuvenation for a woman—something that will aid her in fulfilling her home/life responsibilities. Nevertheless, careful and honest discernment must take place in how much time she can offer to activities that extend her beyond her primary roles as wife and mother. Stein once again confirms this: "It appears to me, however, that there is a limit to such professional activities whenever it jeopardizes domestic life, i.e., the community of life and formation consisting of parents and children."[10]

Overall, because a woman faces an array of seasons through the design of her body (which is stamped with truth) and the choices she makes vocationally, she will encounter life differently than a man. A woman's refusal to acknowledge the seasons will make things difficult because she will be working against her very nature. If a gal denied that it was winter and decided to wear shorts and flip-flops on the coldest day of the year, she'd be really cold! This would be silly and unnecessarily burdensome, even if society told you that you should do it. Weathering the seasons well is important, be it the summer, fall, winter, spring set, or the days of womanhood, which include becoming, singleness, marriage, motherhood, and beyond. Like a poor choice in wardrobe, unbalanced priorities create superfluous stress in a lady's life. A woman truly bears and lives out God's image and design differently than a man, and that's OK. In fact, it is beautiful! Be happy to grow, bud, and bloom just the way you were made, in the many different seasons of your life.

## Chapter Fifteen

### THE MOMENT SHE HAD TOUCHED THEM, THEY ALL FELL ASLEEP
#### ~ *Living Your Faith with Zeal* ~

During high school, there were times in history class (OK, maybe not *just* in history class), that I simply could not keep my eyes open. In those heavy-lidded and bobbing-head moments, it was as if I had been visited by a little fairy who swayed me to sleep with the wave of a wand. To avoid a disciplinary finger being pointed my way, I'd try to shake off sleep, but fatigue usually persisted. The teacher's voice would begin to drone, as I drifted away to the land of "Once Upon a Time." And the reality was that I missed out on some important knowledge. History aside, there is one particular subject worth everyone's wakefulness: Catholicism. Perhaps you think the Church, prayer, or learning about the faith is drab, dry, and dull. If you are having a yawn of a time, you may have a case of Sleeping Beauty Syndrome. It is time to shrug off the sluggishness!

In the story of Sleeping Beauty, the spell of sleep was not a blessing, but a curse. And if you know one thing about your faith, you know God desires to share blessings, not curses, with the faithful! It is the enemy who bestows curses. In *Sleeping Beauty*, the first to go comatose was

Princess Aurora, when she pricked her finger and became dizzy. Who was behind this? None other than Maleficent. Unlike the word *beneficent*, which means, "doing good," *maleficent* signifies "doing evil." She is in stride with Satan. In fact, she calls herself the "mistress of all evil."

Once again, it is time to learn from fairy tales. The truth is, Satan wages war on each of God's faithful. His target is your heart. Why the heart? Countless ink is spilled in Scripture about what dwells in the heart, who is after it, who it was made for, and how to protect it. (Thus, God knew we would need some weaponry for the war waged upon it.) In the chambers of the heart rests the capacity to love, to feel, to pray, to dream, and, most important, to believe: "For man believes with his heart" (Romans 10:10). The heart is the wellspring of life. Without the working heart, the body is dead, and, spiritually speaking, the same is true. "Then the devil comes and takes away the word from their hearts, that they may not believe and be saved" (Luke 8:12). This is precisely why many are asleep. The devil's curse is to hold each heart captive in a sleepy state, keeping God's chosen disengaged and disinterested with the holy. Furthermore, his goal is to prevent us from living a life for God's glory. Someone once said, Satan is like the CIA; he does not want you to know that he exists. Therefore, if he is truly successful, you will not even be actively aware that he is at work—and that your spiritual pulse has flat-lined.

With the enemy's unsolicited help, we have made our faith about something other than love. Many of us are practicing our faith on autopilot. Sleepers may even know a great deal about God's Church, but choose to keep it resting in the mind instead of actively shaping the heart. Such sleepers are neither cold nor hot, and lukewarm is a scary state in which to persist (see Revelation 3:16). Those doomed to dormancy pray halfheartedly and in a state of distraction. If this describes you, and you are simply going through the motions, your heart is unplugged. Jesus said, "For this people's heart has grown dull, / and their ears are heavy of hearing, / and their eyes they have closed, / lest they should perceive with their eyes, / and hear with their ears, / and understand with their heart, / and turn for me to heal them" (Matthew 13:15). To restore your heart, along with your relationship with God, you will need to renew your intimacy with Jesus and ask for his healing. More to come on the subject of revival later.

Another combat tactic of the enemy is to cause and/or capitalize on emotional "heart attacks." The heart suffers pain in any loss: a breakup, an end of a friendship, a death of a family member, a move, and so on. Maybe your heart has lingering feelings of abandonment, lone-liness, rejection, unworthiness, or you feel unlovable; all caused from varying circumstances or traumas. Perhaps you have been emotionally wounded too many times and your heart is worn out. Maybe your heart is pierced because you have given it away again and again, to find love fleeting or not returned. In time, wounds will cause you to place defensive armor upon your heart. Therefore, you may have trouble loving others, even God. Over time, such emotional hardships can cause us to shut down on God. In fact, sometimes we may even hold God responsible. But Jesus is the first place your heart should be. He is the Beloved that will never flee. Putting him second (or third, or fourth) only makes wounds worse. He is the Divine Physician. Your heart belongs in the hands of Christ.

Another way Satan is the thief of hearts is through misplaced adoration. "For where your treasure is, there will your heart be also" (Luke 12:34). If your heart delights in gold, grades, goals, groups of friends, and games of soccer, but is not grounded in God, then you have managed to misplace your heart in false treasures. If you fail to pray and put your heart into him, you have successfully placed small things over the Creator of the Universe! By these false gods our hearts are consumed. We leave no space for God. We forget him, and we grow restless, constantly seeking but never staying satisfied. Funny, in the end, if we rest in Christ, he will also meet our heart's needs. "Take delight in the Lord, / and he will give you the desires of your heart" (Psalm 37:4).

This is war, not just one isolated battle for your heart. In Scripture, countless times the devil tries to take down Christ's followers, but Jesus is there to guard the hearts of his faithful. For example, at the Last Supper, Jesus shares this with St. Peter (who was known as Simon before Christ bestowed on him a new name): "Simon, Simon, behold, Satan demanded to have you, that he might sift you like wheat, but I have prayed for you that your faith may not fail" (Luke 22:31–32). May each of us ask Christ to renew our faith and keep us steadfast in him, that our hearts too may not fail under trials. Jesus has the power to heal us from whatever holds us back from a life aglow with glory.

In *Sleeping Beauty*, Prince Phillip's kiss was the key to awakening the princess from her plague of sleeping death. Your prince, Christ, who is love itself, also has the power to awaken. Jesus rouses hearts and raises the dead. Scripture tells of its very own Sleeping Beauty in the Gospel of Luke:

> And when (Jesus) came to the house, he permitted no one to enter with him, except Peter and John and James, and the father and mother of the child. And all were weeping and bewailing her; but he said, "*Do not weep; for she is not dead but sleeping.*" And they laughed at him, knowing that she was dead. But taking her by the hand he called saying, 'Child, arise.' And her spirit returned, and she got up at once, and he

directed that something should be given her to eat. And her parents were amazed. (Luke 8:51–56, emphasis added)

This was not the only instance of Christ raising someone from the dead. Scripture also tells of Lazarus being raised from the dead after four days in the tomb (see John 11:1–46). But most important of all, Christ rose from the dead himself (see John 20). Death has no power over Jesus! Therefore, if our God has conquered the worst possible curse, death, any other battle we face is a piece of cake for Christ. Jesus said, "In this world you have tribulation; but be of good cheer, I have overcome the world" (John 16:33).

How do you kick start your heart's spiritual cadence? Just like the event quoted above, Jesus's job is the healing, while ours is the asking. In other words, we have to ask Jesus through prayer to come and wake us up. It's time to get out of your jammies! "Awake, O sleeper, and arise from the dead, / and Christ shall give you light" (Ephesians 5:14). Get your pious pulse going with some spiritual exercises on your knees. For "prayer is the surge of the heart" (*CCC* 2558). In prayer, fall for Christ. After all, it is true love's kiss that breaks the curse. "You shall love the Lord your God with all your heart" (Mark 12:30).

The next step toward reviving your heart is reconciliation. Take some time to recall your sins, be serious about amending your life, and get yourself to a confessional. Most Catholic churches offer the sacrament of confession on Saturday afternoons. If you can't make that, you can always make an appointment with a priest. If you are too nervous to go to your local parish, visit another church. The important part is not *where* you go, but *that* you go! Confession can work wonders for your heart. "Interior repentance is a radical reorientation of our whole life, a return, a conversion to God with all our heart" (*CCC* 1431). For, "The whole power of the sacrament of penance consists in restoring us to

God's grace and joining us with him in an intimate friendship" (*CCC* 1468).

Those last words "intimate" and "friendship" are important. Faith should be less about activity and more about intimacy. Empty activity won't help your spiritual life; it will just keep your heart hollow. The Lord says, "You will seek me and find me: when you seek me with all your heart" (Jeremiah 29:13). In other words, put your heart into your faith by searching for Jesus! God makes this promise to you: "A new heart I will give you, and a new spirit I will put within you; and I will take out of your flesh the heart of stone and give you a heart of flesh" (Ezekiel 36:26). It is time say goodnight to your hardened heart and good morning to a happy and holy heart for Christ.

Another way to be intimate with Jesus is by worshipping well. The first step to doing that is getting yourself up for Mass on Sunday—and arriving on time! As a baptized Christian, you have an obligation to attend Mass *every* Sunday. After all, it is a commandment: "Observe the Sabbath day, to keep it holy" (Deuteronomy 5:12). Then, once you are there, don't be a pew potato. Instead, be awake and attentive to what you are doing while worshipping. Also, seek a take away a nugget; something that pops out and sticks with you. Perhaps it is from one of the readings, the homily, a line in a prayer that stands out. In these Mass moments, God is speaking directly to your heart. Take time to listen, for this is part of really being present to Christ. Instead of zoning out, try zoning in! Mass is a divine date. If you went out to coffee with a friend and never made eye contact, and instead only daydreamed and stared down at your shoes, that would be weird. Don't be weird with God.

When Mass begins, make sure your heart is engaged and your body is ready to go. (This might mean arriving a little early in order to get in gear.) Your body is an expression of what is going on in your heart. For example, when a bride and groom kiss, that action is a physical symbol of their heartfelt love. Therefore, bodily actions are outward expressions of interior emotions. Scripture says, "At the name of Jesus, every knee should bow" (Philippians 2:10). When you kneel, kneel like you mean it. What are you saying to Christ with your ups and downs at Mass? Your physical actions should reflect the love that rests in your heart for Christ (or at least the love you want to have). One of the prayers leading up to the consecration of the bread and the wine is: "Lift up your hearts"—and that's exactly what we should be doing. To lift up your heart is to lift it up to heaven. Thus, thoughts should be on heavenly realities instead of drifting back to earthly ones about food, homework, the fabulous skirt you recently purchased, or guys you think are cute. Stay engaged! Once you do, you will find your heart is more and more enthusiastic for Christ.

Keep in mind that Mass is not the only place you meet Christ. Seek to spend time with him outside of your Sunday obligation through prayer. Talk to Christ candidly, not just through formal, scripted words. Tell him about what matters, which means sharing your struggles, dreams, hopes, fears, and longings. You cannot have a real relationship when you are not real with Christ.

Outside of prayer, there are other places you can meet Jesus, too. Part of reviving the heart means you have to restore your vision for the sacred, by allowing yourself time to dwell in beauty. Beauty will help you rediscover God because he is the source of all beauty. Put away all electronic distractions and seek to be with your Creator. Meditate on creation: Sit in the grass, listen to the birds, look at the intricacy of flowers, feel the wind on your face or sand between your toes, or go stargazing. Be in awe of the beauty God has set before you, and allow it to draw your heart deeper.

You will also find beauty and nourishment in the Bible. Therefore, fill your hollow heart with his holy Word (see Luke 8:15). Just flip open a page and see what you find, or go through an entire book of the Bible. "We must rediscover a taste for feeding ourselves the Word of God… offered as sustenance for his disciples."[1] Make a stop into church now and again when it is quiet—just you and Jesus. Have a look around his holy house and admire the statues and stained glass and say a quick hello in prayer. All this will help you not only find your heart, but the Most Sacred Heart. When you do, fix your perpetual dwelling place in the heart of Jesus. Through this act of love, may your heart be found to be in rhythm with his holy heart.

Once you find that your heart is revived, it is time to share! In Scripture, those that were healed couldn't contain themselves (see Matthew 4:23–24; John 9:11). There were even times Jesus told the person he had just healed not to say anything, and they still shared because they were impacted so profoundly (see Mark 1:40–45). If you were just saved through a miraculous encounter, such as a new heart, you might just burst out of the hospital and run through the streets proclaiming your good news. Well, the Gospel is the real Good News. Christianity isn't supposed to be a private thing. Jesus said to his disciples: "Go into all the world and preach the gospel to the whole creation. He who believes and is baptized will be saved; but he who does not believe will be condemned" (Mark 16:15–16). Not only did Christ give us a command to share the faith, he was also pretty clear about what happens to those who do not believe. If we care about anyone in our lives, we should also care about his or her soul. Do we want our loved ones doomed in eternity? Or anyone for that matter? Jesus also said, "Love your neighbor as yourself" (Mark 12:31), and part of loving our neighbors is evangelizing them. Pope Benedict XVI reminds us that "today as in the past, he sends us through the highways of the world to proclaim his Gospel to all the peoples of the earth."[2] We can witness to the world in numerous ways. Here are some ideas to get you started:

First, pray every day and continue to grow in your faith. "Be constant in prayer" (Romans 12:12). If you do not know Christ, you can't help other people get to know him. You have never graduated from God.

Second, put some zeal in your step: "Never flag in zeal, be aglow with the spirit" (Romans 12:11). If you are truly rooted in Christ, this should be the natural result. Jesus is the Savior of the world, therefore we should be excited about it! "The Lord reigns; let the earth rejoice!" (Psalm 97:1). Without Christ's dying for our sins, we would have no life. Therefore, do not be passionless about the Lord's Passion.

Third, live by example. Do not be conformed to the culture, but seek to transform it (see Romans 12:2). St. Francis of Assisi is often quoted as saying, "Preach the Gospel at all times and when necessary, use words." Our actions can be the biggest way to evangelize others. A silent example can be a strong one. If you truly want your actions to reflect Christ in your heart, there are three things you should be doing: (1) Seek to reflect the Gospel with your life; (2) Make sure you do what you say. In other words, do not be a hypocrite. For example, if you say you believe in the Ten Commandments, make your best effort to follow them!; and (3) Don't compartmentalize your faith. An hour on Sunday should not be the only way you showcase your faith. Your belief in Jesus should touch every aspect of your life: the way you dress, speak, play sports, and so on. See others as Christ, making people feel loved by really looking at them (see Romans 12:9), smiling, and being hospitable (see Romans 12:11). Also consider wearing a crucifix or cross as a necklace or ring. This is a great outward sign to show the world that you love God.

Share your faith. For the Christian faith is "a restlessness of consuming fire in the heart to experience the love of Jesus Christ and then share it with others—or it it's nothing at all."[3] Believe boldly enough to have the confidence to share the soul-saving message of Christ. Do not be ashamed of your testimony (see 2 Timothy 1:8). There is no one way to share the Gospel. Look for moments you can have a heart-to-heart with someone about Jesus. If you are not ready to be so direct, think about writing down some Bible verses on a card to share with others when you are out and about. When you grab a coffee, leave the card with the clerk. (You never know how the words of Jesus may touch someone). Order a bundle of medals or holy cards of your favorite saint, and share them with friends or even strangers. Start with gentle nudges.

Sixth, invite your friends or family to Mass. If they say no, give it some time, and then ask again. If they take you up on the offer, be prepared to answer any questions. Also, if you find out someone is a fallen-away Catholic, pass along a bulletin with the Mass times circled, and let them know they are always welcome. You can also invite friends to parish events: talks, youth group nights, and social outings.[4] If your parish doesn't have any events, brainstorm some ideas, pray for God's will to be done, and talk to your pastor about starting something.

With such an important mission ahead of you, you cannot afford to hit the snooze button. Get out of the sleepwalker ranks, and say, "My heart is steadfast, O God, / my heart is steadfast! / I will sing and make melody! / Awake, my soul!" (Psalm 57:7–8). Indeed, the hour has arrived to engage your heart in Christ and to help others to do the same. Bedtime is over, Sleeping Beauty, and the dawn is just beginning. Good morning!

# Chapter Sixteen

## PUT ON THE WHOLE ARMOR OF GOD
### ~ *Knightly Expectations* ~

**Story One:** As I put the finishing touches on my makeup, excitement filled my mind. I was going on my first date. Truth be told, I had orchestrated it. However, I thought that the how of getting what I wanted didn't matter. Once at the restaurant, I sat nervously in the waiting area. Unfortunately, that was the only spot in the restaurant I would see that evening. For an hour, I watched the minute hand make its every tick. Indeed, I was a lady-in-waiting, but I had made it so. There would be no rescue. I had been stood up. I left.

**Story Two:** After some group events, Rob and I really hit it off. My days of arranging dates myself were over. So, I hopefully waited to be asked out. Eventually, he called and asked if I were up for a date. I was thrilled; I would have said yes to fast food. Therefore, when he invited me to meet him in the city, I didn't hesitate to accept his invitation.

Date night arrived, and I got into my car all dressed up, turned on some tunes, and hit the open road—well, more like crowded interstate! Regrettably, I never made it to the date. Due to my horrible navigation skills, I got lost driving in the bad part of town. In my distress, I called to let my date know that I was having a dragon of a time. He was of no help. And after an hour, he gave up on me altogether. It was late. I felt like the darkened city was beginning to consume my car. Clearly, he wouldn't be slaying this dragon for me. Instead, he canceled the date. To make matters worse, I become a demoted damsel, never to be asked out by him again.

**Story Three:** A few months later, I was asked out and picked up for a date by another fellow. I was learning. During our outing, we both seemed to really click. Nevertheless, I wasn't asked out on another date, and I didn't take the hint that he was no longer interested. I thought an explanation on his end was necessary, so I contacted him and demanded to know why. Needless to say, this didn't make him like me any more. I still had a lot to learn.

After those experiences—and a lot of prayer and deliberation—I made a decision. It was time to start acting like the princess, not the prince. I made an oath to myself, and I prayed to God that my husband would rescue me. For despite all my attempted pursuits, deep down I truly longed to be rescued. I realized that if a guy truly liked me, he would be the one to pursue me, plan a date, pick me up, and persist. If he were a gentleman, he would even open doors, and I would let him, even expect him to. In all the fairy tales, the prince finds the princess, right? Wasn't this part of the appeal for the prince—the adventure of finding his love? I was able to let go, and God began opening the doors that needed to be opened, while closing the doors that needed to be closed (just like a gentleman). All the while, I was becoming who I was made to be, a lady.

Scripture is very revealing about God's plan for his children, and so is natural law. Women's bodies were made to welcome, bearing the "gift of receptivity."[1] In other words, in the marital act, a woman's body is made to invite her husband, his body pursuing, her body receiving. However, this is not the only way a woman is receptive. A woman is also receptive emotionally. Since humans are composite beings, made of body and soul, it makes sense that the body impacts a person's emotional and spiritual makeup, as well. For instance, when your body is sick, you just might *feel* like you are physically ugly. Because a woman's body was made to be receptive, her heart is also inclined toward receptivity. Thus, a woman desires not to hunt, but to be romanced and rescued.

Even women's traditional titles shed light on who is called to pursue. A "Miss" or "Mrs." ("Ms." was a later invention) prefaces ladies' last names, whereas men's surnames only appear with a "Mr." It is noteworthy that a woman's title reveals her marital status, while a man's does not. If the expectation were for women to be the seekers, men would have titles that revealed if they were single or not. It again is clear that men are called to be the initiators.

As a woman, the key to helping you find "true love's kiss" is to let yourself be found. That means letting go of the reins and allowing yourself to be pursued. If you go after the guy, there is something missing: his authentic interest. He may be willing to flirt around with the idea of you because he is flattered, but most likely his interest won't last for the long term. However, when a virtuous guy spots you first, he will be determined to meet you, date you, treat you with respect, and, if you are the right girl, marry you.

While you wait in your figurative tower, you have work to do. First, learn to accept who you are, and believe that you are worthy of being found. It is often insecurity in ourselves that makes us pursue men. Pray for confidence. Second, understand that you can't make men "men," so focus on what you can control—yourself. Being rescued doesn't mean you are not capable, it means you are humble, and that you put your full trust in the Lord. These two qualities are just the start of womanly virtues you should seek to possess though living a life rooted in Christ.

On this topic, Bishop Fulton Sheen had this to say: "To a great extent, the level of any civilization is the level of its womanhood. When a man loves a woman, he has to become worthy of her. The higher the virtue, the more her character, the more dedicated she is to truth, justice, goodness, the more a man has to aspire to be worthy of her. The history of civilization could actually be written in terms of the level of its women."[2] Therefore, your control rests in the kind of woman you will be, thus encouraging a man to rise to the challenge of both a life of virtue and a life with you.

Third, spend time praying for your future husband. Pray especially that the Lord will build him in virtue and heal him of vice.

Why is there confusion about what role a woman plays in romance? As mentioned earlier, we are at war. Since the beginning of time the devil, disguised as a serpent, sought to bring down woman in the Garden of Eden, and he continues to seek to destroy (see Revelation 12:13–17). Eve, though innocent, was still capable of sinning because of the gift of free will. We know how the story ends: Eve used her freedom to sin. From that day on, when darkness entered the world, the roles of men and women and their relationship have been confused. Therefore, the "Fallen Eve Syndrome" is something all women have to fight against. Fallen Eve desires to usurp power by seeking control and domination. Fallen Eve is prideful. Why didn't Eve ask Adam to come to her aid when the enemy approached? Moreover, she is good at getting what she wants, even if it isn't very good for her (like poison apples—guys that are not God's desire for her). This is something all women need to fight against as they seek to express true femininity in the way they interact with others. When it comes to dating, this means stepping back and giving "Adam" a chance to pursue you.

During the attack on paradise, men were not left unscathed from sin either. "Fallen Adam Syndrome" leaves men passive, often lacking leadership, and without the desire to protect. Where was Adam when Eve was chatting with Satan? When women seek control, men often willingly hand over the reins. If a guy is too passive to ask you out, don't pursue him. Let him go because true love doesn't begin that way. Plus, a passive guy before marriage means a passive guy *in* marriage.

What began in paradise ages ago is not over. The attack continues. "And the great dragon was thrown down, that ancient serpent, who is called the devil and Satan, the deceiver of the whole world—he was thrown down to the earth, and his angels were thrown down with him" (Revelation 12:9). Today, the fierceness of the devil takes on an even more destructive form; he comes as a dragon. His mission is your demise. Let us not plead ignorance. "The dragon sits by the side of the road, watching those who pass. Beware lest he devour you" (St. Cyril of Jerusalem to catechumens).[3]

What form does this dragon, the devil, take in a lady's life? Scripture can teach us a lot about his tactics. Here are a few descriptive titles: The devil is a deceiver (see Genesis 3:4), an accuser (see Revelation 12:10), our adversary (see 1 Peter 5:8), murderer and liar (see John 8:44). He attacks women physically, intellectually, and morally. Every woman will encounter the dragon differently. Perhaps your dragon is fear in the form of a spider that needs to be stomped by a shoe. Maybe you experience more intense struggles, such as being plagued by emotional or physical burdens. No man will save you from sin but Jesus (see 1 John 3:8). However, a dragon slayer can pray for you and with you, so that you can be strong in the fight.

A true man helps you encounter Christ and supports you in your spiritual journey toward God. A noble knight protects you from harm.

Adam just sat there and watched Satan succeed in introducing sin to Eve. Thus, passive Adam is no knight at all. One great knight of heaven to turn to alone or together is St. Michael the Archangel, who remains a faithful fighter against the dragon (see Revelation 12:7–11).

With the intensity of the battle at hand, it is important to serve God as a faithful princess. Moreover, it is vital to use discernment when dating. Do not settle for a man who is not a true follower of God, and thus unwilling and incapable of facing and defeating dragons. "Fairy tales are more than true—not because they tell us dragons exist, but because they tell us dragons can be beaten."[4] When Sleeping Beauty was cursed, caught, and confined in a tower, the noble prince made his courage known. He too had to face a dragon when Maleficent's true colors were made manifest. However, Prince Phillip did not attempt to approach the enemy unprepared. He came armed in virtue. Your prince should, too.

Here is the scene: Maleficent's evil goblin minions attack Prince Phillip in her fortress. She locks him up in chains and mocks him, attempting to convince him that he is not capable of heroics. The three fairies, Fauna, Flora, and Merryweather, come to his aid. They free Prince Phillip from the chains restraining him and get him suited up. (This scene is very reminiscent of the prison escape of St. Peter, who was helped by an angel. Check it out in Acts 12:4–12.) Next, they tell him that getting to his true love will be dangerous. Together they supply a shield of virtue, a sword of truth, and weapons of righteousness to aid in the battle over evil.[5]

The fairies' actions, advice, and weaponry parallel Scripture, for St. Paul instructs the faithful similarly:

> Be strong in the Lord, and in the strength of his might. Put on the whole armor of God that you may be able to stand against

the wiles of the devil. For we are not contending against flesh and blood, but against the principalities, against the powers, against the world rulers of this present darkness, against the spiritual hosts of wickedness in the heavenly places. Therefore take the whole armor of God, that you may be able to withstand in the evil day, and having done all, to stand. Stand therefore, having girded your loins with *truth*, and having put on the breastplate of *righteousness*, and having shod your feet with the equipment of the gospel of peace; above all taking the shield of faith, with which you can quench all the flaming darts of the evil one. And take the helmet of salvation, and the sword of the Spirit, which is the word of God. (Ephesians 6:10–17, emphasis added).

The devil tries to strip all men of their knighthood, but through daily prayer and faith that noble mission can be restored. Pray for all the men in your life, especially your future spouse! Ask the Lord to dress them in the spiritual armor listed in the verse above. Consider also suiting up similarly in daily prayer. Just because you are a princess doesn't mean you aren't a warrior princess.

One cannot be suited with virtue without God. Your earthly prince should resemble Christ. In other words, he should be less like the *old* Adam and more like Jesus, the *New* Adam. Passive Adam did not rescue Eve. Instead, he sat back and let sin enter the Garden of Eden, whereas Jesus sought to rescue the world through his Passion and death on the cross. "For as in Adam all die, so also in Christ all shall be made alive" (1 Corinthians 15:22). Christ's redemptive suffering begins in a garden, the Garden of Gethsemane (see Matthew 26:36–46). It is as if Jesus is going back to the scene of the crime (the Garden of Eden) where the world's first sin took place. The agony in the garden is the first step toward combat with the devil. Jesus will conquer him on the cross.

So who does *Sleeping Beauty*'s Prince Phillip parallel? It's clear that, like Christ, Prince Phillip is ready to take on the dragon when Maleficent becomes one. Changing from dark enchantress to devilish dragon, she invites the prince to fight against her and the powers of hell.[6] In the concluding battle, as Maleficent casts another curse, a tree springs from the barren earth, which is reminiscent of the Tree of Knowledge of Good and Evil.

The tree quickly grows into an overgrown and knotted thorny hedge. Like Christ, the prince begins his battle in a garden. Thorns neither threaten nor deter him. He faces terror with courage, just as Christ did when the crown of thorns pierced his skull, before the final fight against all the forces of darkness. The secret to prevailing over darkness is fighting under the protection of God. Jesus defeats death by the cross, and so, symbolically, does Prince Phillip, for upon his princely shield is the mark of the cross. As Prince Phillip makes his ultimate and victorious sword throw, we hear a prayer echoed, that by the sword evil would perish and good prevail. The sword pierces the belly of the beast, casting her into the abyss below.[7] With the help of God, evil is always defeated (see Revelation 12:11). Keep your eyes open for a knight who is not afraid to wear his faith on his shield, that is, sleeve.

A true knight will seek to live with virtue. In this way, he is a solider for Christ. Don't settle. Just because a guy got through the door doesn't mean he's your prince. You still need to take it slow and pray. This is the search for *true* love, after all. In a little while, if the guy isn't living up to virtue, he is not a prince.

Don't go entertaining dragons. It's important to instead look for noble characteristics—starting with the most important: prayerfulness.

It is in prayer that he will take on the attributes of Christ. Here are a few other honorable qualities: faithfulness, trustworthiness, kindness, holiness, gentleness, patience, stability, courage, selflessness, compassion, discipline, responsibility, humility, and leadership. Your prince should also be a man that you think would make a good father one day—someone who can show your future daughter how to be treated (by her future prince), and be an example to your sons on how to be real men.

In following these guidelines, and by learning to recognize the qualities of a noble knight, you will find relief and joy in being found—instead of spending your life frantically searching. God designed man to yearn for adventure, and part of that is finding his future bride. And God sculpted your heart with a desire to be sought for with determination. Allow your prince to fight for your heart. Waiting will take patience, but following God's plan for a prince—*your* prince—will save you from not all, but *a lot* of heartache. It takes just one prince to have a match made in heaven. When your prince does come around, you will be ready for marriage, and you'll know he will be, too. You deserve nothing less than to be cherished by a knight of God.

# Conclusion

## HAPPILY EVER AFTER

After the clamor of wedding bells had calmed, and the guests had gone, I was ready to begin my "happily ever after" with my prince on our honeymoon. It was time to ride into the sunset, or in our case, fly toward it, as we journeyed to our tropical destination, St. Lucia.

However, I found out rather quickly that when seeking a happily ever after, there will be bumps in the road—emotional, physical, and spiritual ones. When my new husband and I arrived at the airport for a connecting flight, we soon came to realize, despite our confirmed reservation, we didn't actually have seats on the plane. The airline had overbooked it. We were booted! My expectations of the perfect honeymoon were dashed. We were stuck in Nowhereville. In the end, we made the best of it, and it turned out better than I could have imagined. No matter the circumstances, things won't always be perfect. Keeping off the rose-colored glasses while keeping on the Christ-colored glasses is key!

When planning for whatever happily ever after you have in mind, Christ and his holy Church must be consulted and involved. In reality, your ever after doesn't end with your earthly prince charming, but rather your heavenly one. Marriage is the beginning of a joint journey, where you both seek Christ's dreams for your life and his eternity. The end of Sleeping Beauty's story can remind us of this spiritual reality. Princess Aurora and Prince Phillip ascend toward the heavens as they dance on their wedding day.

In life, we have to fight for the happily ever after. Before poison apples, mean stepsisters, sleeping curses, bad dates, canceled flights, and sin, the world sang a tune of paradise. The Fall led to the fight, but Christ made restoration possible when he died on the cross for our sins, and was resurrected. We only need to embrace and rely on him with all our heart, mind, and soul. Bumps and battles can be expected, but overcome in Christ. Do not lose sight of him. Place your happily ever after in his hands. Also, keep enough fairy dust in your pocket that you don't forget about the fairyland, or the faith lessons, that rest in these pages. It is time to go from sleeping princess to watchful, aware, and prayerful queen. Get ready to for the ball. Wear your crown proudly, and let Christ take the lead on the dance floor of your life.

# Notes

INTRODUCTION
1.  J.R.R. Tolkien, *Tree and Leaf* (London: Harper Collins, 2001), p. 9.
2.  C.S. Lewis, *On Stories and Other Essays on Literature* (New York: Harcourt, 1982), p. 90.

PART ONE
1.  The Brothers Grimm, *Cinderella and Other Tales by the Brothers Grimm* (San Francisco: HarperCollins, 2005), p. 59.

CHAPTER ONE
1.  Brothers Grimm, p. 49.
2.  Brothers Grimm, p. 49.
3.  Brothers Grimm, p. 49.
4.  Philip Schaff, *Jerome: The Principal Works of St. Jerome.*
5.  Fulton J. Sheen, *Three to Get Married* (Princeton, N.J.: Scepter, 1951), p. 12.
6.  Sheen, p. 103.
7.  Fulton J. Sheen, *The World's First Love: A Moving Portrait of the Virgin Mary* (New York: McGraw-Hill, 1952), p. 20.
8.  Christina McShane, "Lovely Lady," *Radiant Magazine.* Spring 2010, p. 13.

CHAPTER TWO
1.  *Snow White and the Seven Dwarfs,* directed by Ben Sharpsteen (Burbank, Calif.: Disney Enterprises, Inc., 1938), DVD.
2.  *Snow White and the Seven Dwarfs.*
3.  Brothers Grimm, p. 60.
4.  Sheen, *The World's First Love,* p. 15.
5.  *Snow White and the Seven Dwarfs.*
6.  Sheen, *Three to Get Married,* p. 4.
7.  Sheen, *Three to Get Married* p. 4.

CHAPTER THREE
1.  Brothers Grimm, p. 51.
2.  Brothers Grimm, p. 51.
3.  *Snow White and the Seven Dwarfs.*
4.  Max Lucado, *Fearless: Imagine Your Life Without Fear* (Nashville: Thomas Nelson, 2009), p. 9.
5.  Lucado, p.13.

CHAPTER FOUR

1. John and Stasi Eldredge, *Captivating: Unveiling the Mystery of a Woman's Soul* (Nashville: Nelson Impact, 2005), p. 11.
2. Germain Grisez and Russell Shaw, *Personal Vocation: God Calls Everyone By Name* (Huntington, Ind.: Our Sunday Visitor, 2003), p. 40, quoting the U.S. bishops' 1992 pastoral letter *Stewardship: A Disciple's Response.*
3. Grisez and Shaw, p. 40.
4. Grisez and Shaw, p. 34.
5. Edith Stein, *The Collected Works of Edith Stein: Essays on Women,* eds. Dr. L. Gelber and Romueus Leuven, O.C.D., Volume II (Washington, D.C.: ICS, 1996), p. 44.
6. Grisez and Shaw, p. 35.
7. Grisez and Shaw, p. 40.
8. Grisez and Shaw, p. 96.

CHAPTER FIVE

1. Brothers Grimm, p. 52.
2. Joseph M. Champlin, "Cohabitating Before Marriage," *Catholic Update,* June 2003.
3. See Jason Evert, *If You Really Loved Me* (Cincinnati: Servant, 2008), pp. 87–88; cf. Bennett, et al., Commitment and the Modern Union."
4. Cf. Bennett, et al., "Commitment and the Modern Union: Assessing the Link Between Premarital Cohabitation and Subsequent Marital Stability," *American Sociological Review* 53:1 (February 1988), 127–138.
5. Evert, pp. 87–88.
6. See Champlin, "Cohabitating Before Marriage."

CHAPTER SIX

1. *Snow White* (1938).
2. John and Stasi Eldredge, *Captivating: Unveiling the Mystery of a Woman's Soul* (Nashville: Nelson Impact, 2005), p. 8.
3. Shaunti and Jeff Feldhahn, *For Men Only: A Straightforward Guide to the Inner Lives of Women* (Colorado Springs: Multnomah, 2006), p. 33.
4. Eldredge and Eldredge, p. 9.
5. Eldredge and Eldredge, p. 129.
6. Feldhahn and Feldhahn, p. 104.
7. Alice Von Hildebrand, *The Privilege of Being a Woman* (Ann Arbor, Mich.: Sapientia, 2005), p. 47.
8. *Mulieris Dignitatem,* 18.
9. John Eldredge, *Wild at Heart: Discovering the Secrets of a Man's Soul* (Nashville: Thomas Nelson, 2001), pp. 8–9.

10. See Shaunti Feldhahn, *For Women Only: What You Need to Know About the Inner Lives of Men* (Colorado Springs: Multnomah, 2004), p. 23.

11. Feldhahn, *For Women Only: What You Need to Know about the Inner Lives of Men* (Colorado Springs: Multnomah, 2013), p. 76.

12. Anne Moir, Ph.D., and David Jessel, *Brain Sex: The Real Difference Between Men and Women,* (New York: Dell, 1989), p. 5.

13. Moir and Jessel, p. 25.

14. Moir and Jessel, p. 37.

15. Von Hildebrand, pp. 76–77.

16. Stein, p. 95.

CHAPTER SEVEN

1. *Kiwi* is slang for a New Zealand native.

2. Brothers Grimm, p. 58.

3. Brothers Grimm, p. 57.

4. Brothers Grimm, p. 58.

5. Brothers Grimm, p. 58.

CHAPTER EIGHT

1. Brothers Grimm, p. 56.

2. Brothers Grimm, p. 57.

3. Kimberly Hahn, *Life Giving Love: Embracing God's Beautiful Design for Marriage* (Cincinnati: Servant, 2001), p. 82.

4. Hahn, p. 67.

5. Teresa Tomeo, Molly Miller, Monica Cops, and Cheryl Dickow, *All Things Girl: Truth for Teens* (Waterford, Mich.: Bezalel, 2009), p. 74.

6. Brothers Grimm, p. 58.

7. http://www.usccb.org/beliefs-and-teachings/what-we-believe/love-and-sexuality/index.cfm#healthcare.

8. Tomeo, et al., p. 75.

9. Hahn, p. 68.

10. *Humanae Vitae*, p. 16.

PART TWO

1. Brothers Grimm, p. 1.

CHAPTER NINE

1. In Latin, *fiat* means "let it be done" or "yes."

2. *Cinderella*, directed by Clyde Geronimi (Burbank, Calif.: Disney Enterprises, Inc., 1950). DVD.

3. Shaunti Feldhahn and Lisa A. Rice, *For Young Women Only: What You Need to Know About How Guys Think* (Colorado Springs: Multnomah, 2006), p. 89.

4. Feldhahn and Rice, p. 89.
5. Feldhahn and Rice, p. 98.
6. Von Hildebrand, p. 90.
7. Brothers Grimm, p. 1.
8. Von Hildebrand, p. 51. Emphasis in original.
9. *Cinderella.*
10. See Von Hildebrand, p. 89.
11. Perrault, *The Blue Fairy Book* (New York: Dover, 1965), p. 66.
12. Perrault, p. 66.
13. Brothers Grimm, p. 3.
14. Brothers Grimm, p. 3.
15. Brothers Grimm, p. 3.
16. Perrault, p. 68.

Chapter Ten

1. John Cuddeback, *Friendship: The Art of Happiness* (Greeley, Colo.: Epic, 2003), p. 7.
2. Philip D. Halfacre, *Genuine Friendship: The Foundation for All Personal Relationships, Including Marriage and the Relationship with God* (Woodridge, Ill.: Midwest Theological Forum, 2008), p. 59.
3. Halfacre, 61.
4. Ruth Sanderson, *Cinderella* (Northampton, Mass.: Crocodile, 2014), p. 4.
5. Halfacre, p. 25.
6. Cuddeback, p. 39.
7. Cuddeback, p. 34.
8. Cuddeback, p. 45.
9. Cuddeback, p. 53.
10. Halfacre, p. 68.
11. Halfacre, p. 69.
12. Cuddeback, p. 28.

Chapter Eleven

1. *Cinderella.*
2. Perrault, p. 68.
3. Sheen, *Three to Get Married*, p. 180.
4. Perrault, p. 69.
5. Justin Lookadoo and Hayley DiMarco, *Dateable: Are You? Are They?*, (Grand Rapids: Fleming H. Revell, 2003), p. 35.
6. Shannon Ethridge and Stephen Arterburn, *Every Young Woman's Battle: Guarding Your Mind, Heart, and Body in a Sex-Saturated World*, (Colorado Springs: Waterbrook, 2004), p. 20.

7. G.K. Chesterton, *All Things Considered* (London: Cox and Wyman, 1969), p. 166.

8. Chesterton, p. 166.

9. Brothers Grimm, pp. 3–4.

10. Brothers Grimm, pp. 3–4.

11. Lookadoo and DiMarco, p. 116.

12. Lookadoo and DiMarco, p. 138.

13. Jason Evert, *If You Really Loved Me: 100 Questions on Dating, Relationships, and Sexual Purity,* (Cincinnati: Servant, 2008), p. 257.

CHAPTER TWELVE

1. Brothers Grimm, p. 5.

2. *Cinderella.*

3. See Beverley Jackson, *Splendid Slippers: A Thousand Years of an Erotic Tradition* (Berkeley, Calif.: Ten Speed, 1997), p. 11.

4. Jackson, p. 18.

5. Brothers Grimm, p. 5.

CHAPTER THIRTEEN

1. *Mulieris Dignitatem,* 21. Emphasis in original.

2. *Cinderella.*

3. Rose is also worn by priests during the third week of Advent for Gaudete Sunday and on Laetare Sunday during Lent; both Latin words mean "rejoice."

4. *Gaudium et Spes,* 48.

5. *Mulieris Dignitatem,* 21.

PART THREE

1. Brothers Grimm, p. 39.

CHAPTER FOURTEEN

1. In fact, the word *Lent* comes from the Old English word *lengten,* which means "spring."

2. *Sleeping Beauty,* directed by Clyde Geronimi (Burbank, Calif.: Disney, 1959), DVD.

3. Thérèse of Lisieux, *Story of a Soul: The Autobiography of St. Therese of Lisieux,* ed. John Clark, third edition (Washington, D.C.: ICS, 1996), p. 14.

4. *Letter to Women,* 2.

5. See Page McKean Zyromski, "Matrimony," *Catechist Magazine,* January 2007, p. 28.

6. Alice Von Hildebrand, *The Privilege of Being a Woman* (Ann Arbor, Mich.: Sapientia, 2005), p. 33.

7. Pope John Paul II, *Familiaris Consortio,* 23.
8. Stein, p. 80.
9. Stein, p. 80.
10. Stein, p. 80.

CHAPTER FIFTEEN

1. *Porta Fidei,* 3.
2. *Porta Fidei,* 3.
3. "Archbishop Chaput: Catholics Should Live Their Faith 'All In,'" *Catholic News Agency,* June 24, 2013, http://www.catholicnewsagency.com.
4. Going together to the event—as opposed to meeting you there—might make them feel less intimidated.

CHAPTER SIXTEEN

1. Von Hildebrand, p. 62.
2. Fulton J. Sheen, *Life Is Worth Living* (San Francisco: Ignatius, 1999), pp. 255, 259.
3. Flannery O'Connor, *Mystery and Manners: Occasional Prose,* Sally Fitzgerald, and Robert Fitzgerald, eds. (New York: Farrar, Straus, and Giroux, 1969), p. 35.
4. G.K. Chesterton as quoted by Neil Gaiman, *Coraline,* revised edition, (New York: HarperCollins, 2012), p. ix.
5. *Sleeping Beauty.*
6. *Sleeping Beauty.*
7. *Sleeping Beauty.*

If you liked *The Princess Guide*, you might also like these:

ISBN 978-0-86716-998-0

ISBN 978-0-86716-921-8

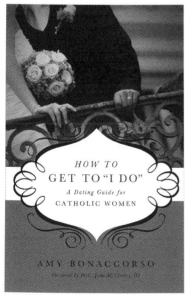

ISBN 978-0-86716-952-2

ISBN 978-1-61636-430-4

ABOUT THE AUTHOR

Jennessa Terraccino has an M.A. in theological studies and an advanced apostolic catechetical diploma from the Christendom College graduate school. She also holds a certificate in youth ministry accredited by Franciscan University of Steubenville. Jennessa served as youth director in the Diocese of Arlington, Virginia. She speaks at conferences and retreats including youth groups, Pure Fashion, and universities. Her articles have appeared in a variety of Catholic publications; this is her first book. Find out more at www.femmeorfaux.com.